T0146449

The Little Book for Dads

The

LITTLE BOOK
for

DADS

STORIES, JOKES,
GAMES, *and* MORE

Avon, Massachusetts

Copyright © 2015 by F+W Media, Inc.
All rights reserved.
This book, or parts thereof, may not be reproduced in any form without permission from
the publisher; exceptions are made for brief excerpts used in published reviews.

Published by
Adams Media, a division of F+W Media, Inc.
57 Littlefield Street, Avon, MA 02322. U.S.A.
www.adamsmedia.com

Contains material adapted and abridged from *The Everything® Mother Goose Book* by June
Rifkin, copyright © 2001 by F+W Media, Inc., ISBN 10: 1-58062-490-1, ISBN 13: 978-1-
58062-490-9; *The Little Book for Boys* by M.L. Stratton, copyright © 2011 by F+W Media,
Inc., ISBN 10: 1-4405-2895-0, ISBN 13: 978-1-4405-2895-8; *The Everything® Pizza Cook-
book* by Belinda Hulin, copyright © 2007 by F+W Media, Inc., ISBN 10: 1-59869-259-3,
ISBN 13: 978-1-59869-259-4; *The Everything® Fairy Tales Book* by Amy Peters, copyright
© 2001 by F+W Media, Inc., ISBN 10: 1-58062-546-0, ISBN 13: 978-1-58062-546-3; *The
Everything® Kids' Soccer Book, 2nd Edition*, by Deborah W. Crisfield, copyright © 2009 by
F+W Media, Inc., ISBN 10: 1-60550-162-X, ISBN 13: 978-1-60550-162-8; *The Everything®
Kids' Football Book, 3rd Edition*, by Greg Jacobs, Reporter/Statistician, STATS, LLC, copy-
right © 2012 by F+W Media, Inc., ISBN 10: 1-4405-4009-8, ISBN 13: 978-1-4405-4009-7;
The Everything® Kids' Baseball Book, 7th Edition, by Greg Jacobs, Reporter/Statistician,
STATS, LLC, copyright © 2012 by F+W Media, Inc., ISBN 10: 1-4405-2843-8, ISBN 13:
978-1-4405-2843-9; *The Everything® Kids' Basketball Book* by Bob Schaller with Coach
Dave Harnish, copyright © 2009 by F+W Media, Inc., ISBN 10: 1-60550-165-4, ISBN 13:
978-1-60550-165-9; *The Everything® Kids' Knock Knock Book* by Aileen Weintraub, copy-
right © 2004 by F+W Media, Inc., ISBN 10: 1-59337-127-6, ISBN 13: 978-1-59337-127-2;
The Everything® Card Games Book by Nikki Katz, copyright © 2004 by F+W Media, Inc.,
ISBN 10: 1-59337-130-6, ISBN 13: 978-1-59337-130-2; *The Everything® Tall Tales, Legends,
& Outrageous Lies Book* by Nat Segaloff, copyright © 2001 by F+W Media, Inc., ISBN
10: 1-58062-514-2, ISBN 13: 978-1-58062-514-2; and *The Everything® Kids' Joke Book* by
Michael Dahl, copyright © 2001 by F+W Media, Inc., ISBN 10: 1-58062-686-6, ISBN 13:
978-1-58062-686-6.

"Aladdin and the Wonderful Lamp" is excerpted from *The Blue Fairy Book* by Andrew
Lang, found at *www.gutenberg.org/ebooks/503*.

"The Prince and the Dragon" is excerpted from *The Crimson Fairy Book* by Andrew Lang,
found at *www.gutenberg.org/ebooks/2435*.

"Blue Beard" is excerpted from *The Fairy Tales of Charles Perrault* by Charles Perrault,
found at *www.gutenberg.org/ebooks/29021*.

"Frère Jacques" is excerpted from *The Book of World Famous Music: Classical, Popular,
and Folk* by James J. Fuld, Dover Publications, Inc. 1995. ISBN: 048628445X.

"Tom Thumb," "Rumpelstiltskin," and "The Elves and the Shoemaker," are excerpted from
Grimms' Fairy Tales by The Brothers Grimm, found at *www.gutenberg.org/ebooks/2591*.

"The Leaping Match" is excerpted from *Hans Andersen's Fairy Tales: First Series* by Hans Christian Andersen, found at *www.gutenberg.org/ebooks/32571*.

"The Land of Counterpane" and "Where Go the Boats?" are excerpted from *A Child's Garden of Verses* by Robert Louis Stevenson, found at *www.gutenberg.org/ebooks/136*.

"To an Insect" is extracted from *The Little Book of Society Verse*, compiled by Claude Moore Fuess and Harold Crawford Stearns, found at *www.bartleby.com/263/115.html*.

ISBN 13: 978-1-5072-1001-7
eISBN 13: 978-1-4405-8787-0

Printed in the United States of America.

10   9   8   7   6   5   4   3   2   1

Library of Congress Cataloging-in-Publication Data

The little book for dads.
    pages cm
  ISBN 978-1-4405-8786-3 (pob) -- ISBN 1-4405-8786-8 (pob) -- ISBN 978-1-4405-8787-0 (ebook) -- ISBN 1-4405-8787-6 (ebook)
1. Amusements--Miscellanea. 2. Games--Miscellanea. 3. Sports--Miscellanea. I. Adams Media
  GV1201.L697 2015
  793--dc23

                    2014043589

Always follow safety and commonsense cooking protocol while using kitchen utensils, operating ovens and stoves, and handling uncooked food. If children are assisting in the preparation of any recipe, they should always be supervised by an adult.

Many of the designations used by manufacturers and sellers to distinguish their products are claimed as trademarks. Where those designations appear in this book and F+W Media, Inc. was aware of a trademark claim, the designations have been printed with initial capital letters.

Cover design by Frank Rivera and Erin Alexander.
Cover images © Clipart.com.
Interior images © Clipart.com, 123RF, and iStockphoto.com.

This book is available at quantity discounts for bulk purchases.
For information, please call 1-800-289-0963.

"Anyone can be a father, but it takes someone special to be a dad."

—UNKNOWN

INTRODUCTION

The time you spend with your kids while they're young is so precious and fleeting. Make the most of it with *The Little Book for Dads*! It's the perfect collection of timeless tidbits for you to share with your children. After all, some of your kids' favorite childhood memories will come from the many things you teach them as you play, talk, and snuggle together:

- *The best way to tie a fishing lure.*
- *How to play Kick the Can.*
- *Baseball's greatest all-time players.*
- *Bedtime stories filled with adventure.*

On these pages, you'll find a top-notch collection of jokes, sports lore, silly songs, hands-on activities, stories, and more—all of which help create magical memories your children will remember forever. Whether it's the rules of Crazy Eights, a fun song to sing when you're stuck in traffic, or a bedtime story to send your little ones off to sleep, you'll turn to this treasury again and again.

Take Me Out to the Ball Game

BY JACK NORWORTH AND ALBERT VON TILZER, 1908

Take me out to the ball game,
Take me out with the crowd.
Buy me some peanuts and Cracker Jack,
I don't care if I never get back.
Let me root, root, root for the home team,
If they don't win, it's a shame.
For it's one, two, three strikes, you're out,
At the old ball game.

Hot Cross Buns

Hot cross buns!
Hot cross buns!
One a penny, two a penny,
Hot cross buns!

If you have no daughters,
Give them to your sons.
One a penny, two a penny,
Hot cross buns!

One, Two, Buckle My Shoe

One, two, buckle my shoe;
Three, four, knock at the door;
Five, six, pick up sticks;
Seven, eight, lay them straight;
Nine, ten, a big, fat hen;
Eleven, twelve, dig and delve;
Thirteen, fourteen, maids a-courting;
Fifteen, sixteen, maids in the kitchen;
Seventeen, eighteen, maids a-waiting;
Nineteen, twenty, my plate's empty.

HOW TO MAKE A TIN-CAN TELEPHONE

This nostalgic craft is simple to make and fun to play with. Get ready for hours of entertainment and ingenuity with your tin-can telephone! Now you're talking!

WHAT YOU'LL NEED:

Two tin cans, washed with the paper removed (be careful of sharp edges)

A piece of string

A hammer and a nail (and an adult!)

1. Turn the cans so the solid bottom is at the top. With the hammer and nail, make a hole in the bottom of each can just big enough for the string to get through.
2. Insert the string into each hole. Knot each end of the string inside each can.
3. Pull the string taut so that the knot is right up against the bottom of each can.
4. Now you can speak into one can while someone listens on the other end. The sound of your voice will vibrate across the string and into the other person's ear!

SOCCER SKILL GAMES

MONKEY IN THE MIDDLE

If you have three people, try this version of a good old-fashioned game of Monkey in the Middle. Two of you team up and try to keep possession of the ball while passing it back and forth. The third person does her best to get it away from you.

"CATCH"

Pass the ball back and forth with your child. It's like playing catch, but with a soccer ball! Start by using two touches: you'll "catch" the ball first and then pass it. Once you feel comfortable with that, you can graduate to one-touch passing. See how many times the ball can go back and forth accurately.

SOCCER GOLF

To play soccer golf, you first need a "golf" course. That doesn't mean you rush over to the local course and invade it with your soccer balls. You have to be creative. Go to a park and find "holes," such as a tree, a fountain, a seesaw, and a statue. Play as many "holes" as you like.

Once your course is set up, it's time to play. You and your child should both have a soccer ball. It's also handy to have a pencil and a piece of paper to keep score unless you have a really good memory. The first player "tees off" by kicking the soccer ball toward the goal. Then the next player goes. Count how many kicks it takes to hit the hole. Write that down as your score for that hole. At the end of your course, the player with the lowest score is the winner.

DOUBLE JEOPARDY

This is a good passing game for four players. Have two players line up on one line and two others stand across from them at a good passing distance for your level. Use two balls, one on each side. Now start passing the ball back and forth. The team who can get both balls on one side is the winner.

RED LIGHT, GREEN LIGHT

Red Light, Green Light has always been a great kids' game, and you and your kids can play it with a soccer ball as well. One person is the "traffic light" at the far end of the field. The rest are the "cars." They each have a ball. The player at the far end yells, "Green light!" and turns around. The cars all begin dribbling their balls until they hear the traffic light yell, "Red light!" at which point they all must put a foot on the ball. If any players can't put their foot on the ball because it's too far away from them, then they're sent back to the beginning. The winner (and next traffic light) is the player who crosses the field first. This really teaches you to keep the ball close yet still dribble quickly.

"Before I got married I had six theories about raising children; now, I have six children and no theories."

—JOHN WILMOT

CLASSIC CARD GAME: CRAZY EIGHTS

Looking for a strategy game to play with your little ones? Crazy Eights involves thinking ahead and planning for your last discard. It also develops matching skills, following suit, and recognizing the value of cards.

OBJECTIVE:

To be the first person to discard all of the cards in your hand.

WHAT YOU'LL NEED:

Two or more players are needed to play this game, and you'll use a standard pack of fifty-two cards.

1. A dealer is randomly selected and deals five cards face down to each player, if there are more than two players, or seven cards if there are only two players. The remaining cards are then placed face down in a stockpile, accessible to everyone in the playing area. The top card is turned face up and placed next to the stack of cards to start the discard pile.

2. The game begins with the player to the dealer's left. If the first card turned over in the discard pile is an eight, the player chooses a suit and then discards a card of that suit from his hand. If the card is not an eight, the player discards a card of that suit or of that value from her hand. For instance, if the top card is 6♦, you may discard a six of any suit or any diamond.

3. If you have an eight in your hand, you might want to save it until the last card. This strategy assures that you will be able to discard your last card without having to wait for a suit or value to match that card.

4. If you have no cards that can be played, you must pick up the top card from the stockpile. The next player to the left then plays, with the same options. If you discard an eight, you must then call out a new suit for the next player to play. The game stops when any player discards the last card in her hand.

FOOTBALL TERMS TO KNOW

When you watch sports games with your kids, they might want to know what certain terms mean so they can follow along. Here's a glossary of key football words.

BLITZ In a regular football game, a "blitz" just means that the defense sends a LOT of players to try to tackle the quarterback. In a playground game with a rush count, though, a blitz just means the defense can rush without counting. Many playground games put a limit on how many times the defense can blitz.

DEFENSE The team of eleven players without the ball is the defense. They try to tackle the offensive player with the ball, and they try to knock down or intercept passes.

DOWN Whether they run or pass, the offense has to keep moving if they want to keep the ball. They have four plays, called downs, to advance 10 yards. If they make the 10 yards, they are awarded a first down, and they keep the ball. If they don't get those 10 yards, then the defense gets the ball.

FIELD GOAL Three points scored by kicking the ball through the goalposts.

HOLDING Neither offensive nor defensive players are ever allowed to hold a player who doesn't have the ball. This means no jersey grabbing, hugging, or tackling. Holding usually results in a 10-yard penalty. (Of course, the defense is supposed to do these things to the person who's carrying the ball!)

LINE OF SCRIMMAGE The line of scrimmage is where the referee places the ball at the beginning of a play. Neither the offense nor the defense is allowed to cross the line before the ball is snapped and the action begins. Forward passes may only be thrown from behind the line of scrimmage.

OFFENSE The team of eleven players that controls the ball is the offense. They try to run or pass the ball down the field toward the end zone.

PASS INTERFERENCE When a pass is in the air, the defense can't make contact with the receivers. If they do, the penalty is called pass interference, and it usually costs 15 yards—sometimes even more in the NFL.

POCKET When the quarterback has dropped back to pass, his offensive line forms a horseshoe-shaped pocket around him. They push the pass rushers toward the sideline and down the field, keeping the area around the quarterback clear of defenders until the quarterback can throw a pass.

SACK When the defense tackles the quarterback before he has a chance to pass the ball, that's called a sack. Bruce Smith, who played most of his career for the Buffalo Bills, sacked the quarterback 200 times and holds the all-time NFL record.

SCREEN PASS When the offensive line forms a pocket and the receivers run downfield, the defense is ready for a long pass. Sometimes they forget about the running back. In one common screen pass, the running back and some linemen pretend to miss their blocks so the pass rushers think they can tackle the quarterback. Then the quarterback throws a short pass over the rushers to the running back, who now has a clear field in front of him for a long gain.

TOUCHDOWN Six points. Run the ball into the end zone or catch the ball in the end zone.

HOW TO MAKE AN INSECT HABITAT

*There's nothing more quintessential for kids than explor-
ing the world of insects, and creating an insect habitat will
make hunting for critters with your family even more fun!*

WHAT YOU'LL NEED:

Something to put your little creatures in. (If you don't have a container specifically for insect hunting, any clear plastic container with
a lid will work well. Just be sure to poke holes in the container or lid.
You can also use a clear plastic produce container from the market, provided the insects you catch are not smaller than the holes.)
You'll need to create an environment that will be comfortable for your insects to live in.

1. Collect moss, grass, sticks, leaves, dirt, and rocks for your habitat.
   You'll want to put water in the habitat, too; a small container, like a bottle cap, filled with water will be sufficient.
2. Now it's time to go on an insect hunt! Look near grass, trees, or bushes;
   under rocks; or near gardens, lakes, and ponds. Insects are everywhere.
   You can use a small net or your hands to catch them.
3. Gently place insects in the habitat you've made.
4. Have fun observing your insects and identifying them. Don't forget to
   release them back into the wild when you're finished observing them!

The Prince and the Dragon

FROM *VOLKSMAREHEN DER SERBEN*

O NCE UPON A TIME there lived an emperor who had three sons. They were all fine young men, and fond of hunting, and scarcely a day passed without one or other of them going out to look for game.

One morning the eldest of the three princes mounted his horse and set out for a neighboring forest, where wild animals of all sorts were to be found. He had not long left the castle, when a hare sprang out of a thicket and dashed across the road in front. The young man gave chase at once, and pursued it over hill and dale, till at last the hare took refuge in a mill which was standing by the side of a river. The prince followed and entered the mill, but stopped in terror by the door, for, instead of a hare, before him stood a dragon, breathing fire and flame. At this fearful sight the prince turned to fly, but a fiery tongue coiled round his waist, and drew him into the dragon's mouth, and he was seen no more.

A week passed away, and when the prince never came back everyone in the town began to grow uneasy. At last his next brother told the emperor that he likewise would go out to hunt, and that perhaps he would find some clue as to his brother's disappearance. But hardly had the castle gates closed on the prince than the hare sprang out of the bushes as before, and led the huntsman up hill and down dale, till they reached the mill. Into this the hare flew with the prince at his heels, when, lo! instead of the hare, there stood a dragon breathing fire and flame; and out shot a fiery tongue which coiled round the prince's waist, and lifted him straight into the dragon's mouth, and he was seen no more.

Days went by, and the emperor waited and waited for the sons who never came, and he could not sleep at night for wondering where they were and what had become of them. His youngest son wished to go in search of his brothers, but for a long time the emperor refused to listen to him, lest he should lose him also. But the prince prayed so hard for leave to make the search, and promised so often that he would be very cautious and careful, that at length the emperor gave him permission, and ordered the best horse in the stables to be saddled for him.

Full of hope the young prince started on his way, but no sooner was he outside the city walls than a hare sprang out of the bushes and ran before him, till they reached the mill. As before, the animal dashed in through the open door, but this time he was not followed by the prince. Wiser than his brothers, the young man turned away, saying to himself: "There are as good hares in the forest as any that have come out of it, and when I have caught them, I can come back and look for you."

For many hours he rode up and down the mountain, but saw nothing, and at last, tired of waiting, he went back to the mill. Here he found an old woman sitting, whom he greeted pleasantly.

"Good morning to you, little mother," he said; and the old woman answered: "Good morning, my son."

"Tell me, little mother," went on the prince, "where shall I find my hare?"

"My son," replied the old woman, "that was no hare, but a dragon who has led many men hither, and then has eaten them all." At these words the prince's heart grew heavy, and he cried, "Then my brothers must have come here, and have been eaten by the dragon!"

"You have guessed right," answered the old woman; "and I can give you no better counsel than to go home at once, before the same fate overtakes you."

"Will you not come with me out of this dreadful place?" said the young man.

"He took me prisoner, too," answered she, "and I cannot shake off his chains."

"Then listen to me," cried the prince. "When the dragon comes back, ask him where he always goes when he leaves here, and what makes him so strong; and when you have coaxed the secret from him, tell me the next time I come."

So the prince went home, and the old woman remained in the mill, and as soon as the dragon returned she said to him:

"Where have you been all this time—you must have traveled far?"

"Yes, little mother, I have indeed traveled far," answered he. Then the old woman began to flatter him, and to praise his cleverness; and when she thought she had got him into a good temper, she said: "I have wondered so often where you get your strength from; I do wish you would tell me. I would stoop and kiss the place out of pure love!" The dragon laughed at this, and answered:

"In the hearthstone yonder lies the secret of my strength."

Then the old woman jumped up and kissed the hearth; whereat the dragon laughed the more, and said:

"You foolish creature! I was only jesting. It is not in the hearthstone, but in that tall tree that lies the secret of my strength." Then the old woman jumped up again and put her arms round the tree, and kissed it heartily. Loudly laughed the dragon when he saw what she was doing.

"Old fool," he cried, as soon as he could speak, "did you really believe that my strength came from that tree?"

"Where is it then?" asked the old woman, rather crossly, for she did not like being made fun of.

"My strength," replied the dragon, "lies far away; so far that you could never reach it. Far, far from here is a kingdom, and by its capital city is a lake, and in the lake is a dragon, and inside the dragon is a wild boar, and inside the wild boar is a pigeon, and inside the pigeon a sparrow, and inside the sparrow is my strength." And when the old woman heard this, she thought it was no use flattering him any longer, for never, never, could she take his strength from him.

The following morning, when the dragon had left the mill, the prince came back, and the old woman told him all that the creature had said. He listened in silence, and then returned to the castle, where he put on a suit of shepherd's clothes, and taking a staff in his hand, he went forth to seek a place as tender of sheep.

For some time he wandered from village to village and from town to town, till he came at length to a large city in a distant kingdom, surrounded on three sides by a great lake, which happened to be the very lake in which the dragon lived. As was his custom, he stopped everybody whom he met in the streets that looked likely to want a shepherd and begged them to engage him, but they all seemed to have shepherds of their own, or else not to need any. The prince was beginning to lose heart, when a man who had overheard his question turned round and said that he had better go and ask the emperor, as he was in search of some one to see after his flocks.

"Will you take care of my sheep?" said the emperor, when the young man knelt before him.

"Most willingly, your Majesty," answered the young man, and he listened obediently while the emperor told him what he was to do.

"Outside the city walls," went on the emperor, "you will find a large lake, and by its banks lie the richest meadows in my kingdom. When you are leading out your flocks to pasture, they will all run straight to these meadows, and none that have gone there have ever been known to come back. Take heed, therefore, my son, not to suffer your sheep to go where they will, but drive them to any spot that you think best."

With a low bow the prince thanked the emperor for his warning, and promised to do his best to keep the sheep safe. Then he left the palace and went to the marketplace, where he bought two greyhounds, a hawk, and a set of pipes; after that he took the sheep out to pasture.

The instant the animals caught sight of the lake lying before them, they trotted off as fast as their legs would go to the green meadows lying round it. The prince did not try to stop them; he only placed his hawk on the branch of a tree, laid his pipes on the grass, and bade the greyhounds sit still; then, rolling up his sleeves and trousers, he waded into the water crying as he did so: "Dragon! Dragon! If you are not a coward, come out and fight with me!" And a voice answered from the depths of the lake:

"I am waiting for you, O prince"; and the next minute the dragon reared himself out of the water, huge and horrible to see. The prince sprang upon him and they grappled with each other and fought together till the sun was high, and it was noonday. Then the dragon gasped:

"O prince, let me dip my burning head once into the lake, and I will hurl you up to the top of the sky." But the prince answered, "Oh, ho! My good dragon, do not crow too soon! If the emperor's daughter were only here, and would kiss me on the forehead, I would throw you up higher still!" And suddenly the dragon's hold loosened, and he fell back into the lake.

As soon as it was evening, the prince washed away all signs of the fight, took his hawk upon his shoulder, and his pipes under his arm, and with his greyhounds in front and his flock following after him he set out for the city. As they all passed through the streets the people stared in wonder, for never before had any flock returned from the lake.

The next morning he rose early, and led his sheep down the road to the lake. This time, however, the emperor sent two men on horseback to ride behind him, with orders to watch the prince all day long. The horsemen kept the prince and his sheep in sight, without being seen themselves. As soon as they beheld the sheep running towards the meadows, they turned aside up a steep hill, which overhung the lake. When the shepherd reached the place he laid, as before, his pipes on the grass and bade the greyhounds sit beside them, while the hawk he perched on the branch of the tree. Then he rolled up his trousers and his sleeves, and waded into the water crying:

"Dragon! Dragon! If you are not a coward, come out and fight with me!" And the dragon answered:

"I am waiting for you, O prince," and the next minute he reared himself out of the water, huge and horrible to see. Again they clasped each other tight round the body and fought till it was noon, and when the sun was at its hottest, the dragon gasped:

"O prince, let me dip my burning head once in the lake, and I will hurl you up to the top of the sky." But the prince answered:

"Oh, ho! My good dragon, do not crow too soon! If the emperor's daughter were only here, and would kiss me on the forehead, I would throw you up higher still!" And suddenly the dragon's hold loosened, and he fell back into the lake.

As soon as it was evening the prince again collected his sheep, and playing on his pipes he marched before them into the city. When he passed through the gates all the people came out of their houses to stare in wonder, for never before had any flock returned from the lake.

Meanwhile the two horsemen had ridden quickly back, and told the emperor all that they had seen and heard. The emperor listened eagerly to their tale, then called his daughter to him and repeated it to her.

"Tomorrow," he said, when he had finished, "you shall go with the shepherd to the lake, and then you shall kiss him on the forehead as he wishes."

But when the princess heard these words, she burst into tears, and sobbed out:

"Will you really send me, your only child, to that dreadful place, from which most likely I shall never come back?"

"Fear nothing, my little daughter, all will be well. Many shepherds have gone to that lake and none have ever returned; but this one has in these two days fought twice with the dragon and has escaped without a wound. So I hope tomorrow he will kill the dragon altogether, and deliver this land from the monster who has slain so many of our bravest men."

Scarcely had the sun begun to peep over the hills next morning, when the princess stood by the shepherd's side, ready to go to the lake. The shepherd was brimming over with joy, but the princess only wept bitterly. "Dry your tears, I implore you," said he. "If you will just do what I ask you, and when the time comes, run and kiss my forehead, you have nothing to fear."

Merrily the shepherd blew on his pipes as he marched at the head of his flock, only stopping every now and then to say to the weeping girl at his side:

"Do not cry so, Heart of Gold; trust me and fear nothing." And so they reached the lake.

In an instant the sheep were scattered all over the meadows, and the prince placed his hawk on the tree, and his pipes on the grass, while he bade his greyhounds lie beside them. Then he rolled up his trousers and his sleeves, and waded into the water, calling:

"Dragon! Dragon! If you are not a coward, come forth, and let us have one more fight together." And the dragon answered: "I am waiting for you, O prince"; and the next minute he reared himself out of the water, huge and horrible to see. Swiftly he drew near to the bank, and the prince sprang to meet him, and they grasped each other round the body and fought till it was noon. And when the sun was at its hottest, the dragon cried:

"O prince, let me dip my burning head in the lake, and I will hurl you to the top of the sky." But the prince answered:

"Oh, ho! My good dragon, do not crow too soon! If the emperor's daughter were only here, and she would kiss my forehead, I would throw you higher still."

Hardly had he spoken, when the princess, who had been listening, ran up and kissed him on the forehead. Then the prince swung the dragon straight up into the clouds, and when he touched the earth again, he broke into a thousand pieces. Out of the pieces there sprang a wild boar and galloped away, but the prince called his hounds to give chase, and they caught the boar and tore it to bits. Out of the pieces there sprang a hare, and in a moment the greyhounds were after it, and they caught it and killed it; and out of the hare there came a pigeon. Quickly the prince let loose his hawk, which soared straight into the air, then swooped upon the bird and brought it to his master. The prince cut open its body and found the sparrow inside, as the old woman had said.

"Now," cried the prince, holding the sparrow in his hand, "now you shall tell me where I can find my brothers."

"Do not hurt me," answered the sparrow, "and I will tell you with all my heart. Behind your father's castle stands a mill, and in the mill are three slender twigs. Cut off these twigs and strike their roots with them, and the iron door of a cellar will open. In the cellar you will find as many people, young and old, women and children, as would fill a kingdom, and among them are your brothers."

By this time twilight had fallen, so the prince washed himself in the lake, took the hawk on his shoulder and the pipes under his arm, and with his greyhounds before him and his flock behind him, marched gaily into the town, the princess following them all, still trembling with fright. And so they passed through the streets, thronged with a wondering crowd, till they reached the castle.

Unknown to anyone, the emperor had stolen out on horseback, and had hidden himself on the hill, where he could see all that happened. When all was over, and the power of the dragon was broken for ever, he rode quickly back to the castle, and was ready to receive the prince with open arms, and to promise him his daughter to wife. The wedding took place with great splendor, and for a whole week the town was hung with colored lamps, and tables were spread in the hall of the castle for all who chose to come and eat. And when the feast was over, the prince told the emperor and the people who he really was, and at this everyone rejoiced still more, and preparations were made for the prince and princess to return to their own kingdom, for the prince was impatient to set free his brothers.

The first thing he did when he reached his native country was to hasten to the mill, where he found the three twigs as the sparrow had told him. The moment that he struck the root the iron door flew open, and from the cellar a countless multitude of men and women streamed forth. He bade them go one by one wheresoever they would, while he himself waited by the door till his brothers passed through. How delighted they were to meet again, and to hear all that the prince had done to deliver them from their enchantment. And they went home with him and served him all the days of their lives, for they said that he only who had proved himself brave and faithful was fit to be king.

ALL-TIME BASKETBALL GREATS

Whether your kids just shoot hoops in the driveway or aspire to be the next Michael Jordan, it's fun to remember some of basketball's best players.

KAREEM ABDUL-JABBAR

Kareem, who was born Ferdinand Lewis Alcindor but changed his name, was drafted by the Milwaukee Bucks after a great career at UCLA under legendary coach John Wooden, where he won three straight collegiate championships. Kareem, who was rookie of the year, played until age 42 and has held records for points scored, shots blocked, most seasons played, most NBA Most Valuable Player Awards (6), and the most all-star games (18). Even though he was over seven feet tall, he was still graceful and quick. Defenders were powerless to stop his "Skyhook" shot. Kareem helped his teams win six NBA Championships.

LARRY BIRD

Larry Bird did everything well. He passed, rebounded, shot, played defense—and won. Larry brought out the best in his teammates and the result was three NBA championships as the face of the Celtics from 1979–1991. He was always at his best when important games were on the line. Larry was a 12-time All-Star Team selection. He was also good at the fundamentals, leading the league four times in free-throw percentage. During one streak in his career, Larry made 71 free throws in a row. Larry won a gold medal with the Dream Team in the 1992 Olympics.

WILT CHAMBERLAIN

Wilt "The Stilt" Chamberlain was seen as the most powerful offensive player in the game. He was a dominant figure at 7 feet 1 inch tall and 300 pounds. He was the only player to score 4,000 points in a season. He scored 100 points for the Philadelphia Warriors in a victory against the Knicks in 1962. He also set an NBA record with 55 rebounds in one game. Wilt was a defensive force, leading the league in rebounding 11 of the 14 seasons he played. He could also pass, leading the league in assists in 1967–1968.

JULIUS ERVING

He was known as "Dr. J," and before Michael Jordan came into the league, Julius Erving was the player with the high-flying dunks. In the five ABA seasons he played, 1971–1976, he won three scoring titles, three Most Valuable Player awards, and two ABA championships. He was an All-Star all 11 years he played in the NBA, 1977–1987, and he was clearly the most dominating offense player of his era. Julius was the most respected player of his time and he always conducted himself as an ambassador for the league. He was NBA MVP in 1981 and led Philadelphia to the NBA title in 1983. At 6 feet 7 inches, Julius would glide to the basket for his famous one-handed dunks.

EARVIN "MAGIC" JOHNSON

At 6 feet 9 inches, it was hard to imagine Magic Johnson as a point guard. Yet he revolutionized the game with his no-look passes and also pulled down more than seven rebounds a game. Though his shooting skills were never given a lot of respect, he averaged 19.5 points a game during his distinguished career. Magic led Los Angeles to five NBA titles and set the standard for rivalry with classic matchups with Larry Bird and the Boston Celtics. Magic was the king of the triple double—double figures in points, rebounds, and assists. He also won an Olympic gold medal with the original Dream Team in 1992.

MICHAEL JORDAN

Ask almost anyone who the best NBA player of all time was, and Michael Jordan is usually the first name mentioned. The 6-feet-5-inch Michael was a five-time NBA MVP who redefined the offense game. He scored seemingly at will, defied gravity with a variety of dunks, and—perhaps most importantly—made all the players around him better. Michael and his teammates in the Chicago Bulls won six NBA titles. As a player, Michael had few peers; he was too tall for a guard to defend but too fast and too good of a shooter for a forward to try to stop. Though "His Airness" was known for his high-flying dunks, he was also named the league's best defensive player and was a constant on the All-Defensive team. Michael won three NBA titles in a row in 1991, 1992, and 1993. After the 1993 season, he announced he was trading in his high tops for baseball cleats but rejoined the Bulls in the middle of the 1994–1995 season and led the Bulls to another three-peat, winning the NBA championship in 1996, 1997, and 1998. Michael made his decision to retire a second time in 1999. Though he will always be known as a Chicago Bulls star, Michael came out of retirement and played two additional seasons (2001–2002 and 2002–2003) for the Washington Wizards before retiring once and for all.

HAKEEM OLAJUWON

Hakeem "The Dream" Olajuwon led the Houston Rockets to their first two titles in NBA history. In 1993–1994, he won the league Most

Valuable Player Award and the NBA Finals MVP honor while leading Houston to its first NBA championship. He followed that up with a spot on the 1996 U.S. Olympic Dream Team, which won a gold medal in Atlanta. For his size, Hakeem had surprising agility and a soft touch shooting the basketball and he developed a wide array of offensive shots, including spin moves and fade-away jump shots. He averaged 26 points or more per game for four seasons in a row. He was also a defensive force, winning the Defensive Player of the Year award in 1993.

BILL RUSSELL

As a college player at San Francisco, Bill Russell led his team to two NCAA championships—in 1955 and 1956—though he was forced to miss the final four games of the 1956 NCAA tournament because his college eligibility had expired. Bill still made an important appearance in a championship game in 1956, when he led the U.S. Olympic Basketball Team to a gold medal at the Olympics. Bill was a defensive power, changing the game of basketball by blocking shots. He also had 21,620 rebounds during his career, an average of 22.5 rebounds a game, a huge number that hasn't been matched since. Above all, Bill was regarded as the ultimate team player and a winner. He led the Celtics to 11 NBA Championships in his 13 seasons.

MEAT-LOVERS' PIZZA

This hearty pizza isn't for the faint of heart. Serve it on a cold day with forks and plenty of napkins.

MAKES TWO 12" PIZZAS

Enough dough for two 12" pizzas
2 pounds sliced mozzarella cheese
4 cups tomato sauce
½ pound ground beef, browned

½ pound bulk sausage, browned
½ pound finely diced ham
½ pound finely diced pepperoni
2 cups shredded Parmesan cheese

1. Coat two 12" deep-dish pizza or pie pans with olive oil. Divide dough and press into pans, making sure dough goes all the way up the sides of the pans. Preheat oven to 450°F.
2. Lay mozzarella slices over the crust of each pizza, using about half the mozzarella. Pour 1½ cups sauce in the center of each pizza and spread evenly over the mozzarella. Sprinkle the meats, in the order listed, evenly over the sauce.
3. Lay remaining mozzarella slices evenly over the meats. Spread remaining sauce over the cheese layer, dividing evenly over the two pizzas.
4. Sprinkle 1 cup Parmesan over the top of each pizza.
5. Reduce heat to 400°F and bake pizzas for 20–25 minutes or until crust is light brown and centers are browned and bubbly.

American Legends

DANIEL BOONE (1734–1820)

Daniel Boone was very much a pioneer. Following the French and Indian War of 1756, Pennsylvania-born Boone went through the Cumberland Gap and saw a lake containing a large salt lick (the significance of this salt lick is that it attracted a huge amount of game). The region had been declared off-limits to colonists by a 1763 decree from King George III, but when news of Boone's discovery "leaked" to whites, the scramble incited feuds among resident Native American tribes. By 1773, Boone was leading settlement parties through the Cumberland Gap, which some Native Americans called "Kentucke," further displacing the original residents.

PAUL BUNYAN

Fabled woodsman Paul Bunyan, who traveled the forests of the northern United States with Babe, his blue ox (blue because Bunyan discovered him nearly frozen in the snow), is a staple of the American landscape. He stands guard over diners, lumber yards, and miniature golf courses. Going as far back as maybe even the eighteenth century, Bunyan's legend was introduced to a wide audience in 1914 when advertising manager W.B. Laughead created a sales brochure for the Red River Lumber Company of Minneapolis, Minnesota. Bunyan was further popularized in a 1958 Disney animated short film.

DAVY CROCKETT (1786–1836)

Davy Crockett was a renowned storyteller, but what is remarkable about his legend is that the broad strokes of it are true. He ingratiated himself to one and all as a good ol' boy by telling folksy tales, many of which he saw fit to write down in almanacs, which means that he was literate. Crockett ran for Congress and won in 1827 and, once in Washington, became known more as a humorist than a politician. After two terms he "lit out" to Texas, where he heard of a fight raging between a Mexican general and some American squatters who refused to surrender a building they were occupying in San Antonio. Thus did Davy Crockett, a Tennessean, die giving birth to Texas—and his own legend—at the Alamo.

The Cat and the Fiddle

Hey, diddle, diddle,
The cat and the fiddle,
The cow jumped over the moon;
The little dog laughed
To see such sport,
And the dish ran away with the spoon.

Dapple-Gray

I had a little pony,
His name was Dapple-Gray,
I lent him to a lady,
To ride a mile away.
She whipped him, she slashed him,
She rode him through the mire;
I would not lend my pony now
For all the lady's hire.

Peter Piper

Peter Piper picked a peck of pickled peppers;
A peck of pickled peppers Peter Piper picked.
If Peter Piper picked a peck of pickled peppers,
Where's the peck of pickled peppers Peter Piper picked?

JUST FOR LAUGHS

Knock knock!

Who's there?

Erma.

Erma who?

Erma going to tell you lots of knock-knock jokes!

Who's there?

Parkway.

Parkway who?

Parkway over there!

Knock knock!

Who's there?

Quack.

Quack who?

Quack another bad joke and I'm leaving!

Knock knock!

Who's there?

Farmer.

Farmer who?

Farmer birthday I'm getting a new bike!

Knock knock!

Who's there?

Thumb.

Thumb who?

Thumb body is at the door!

Knock knock!
Who's there?
Dozen.
Dozen who?
Dozen anyone know?

Knock knock!
Who's there?
Daisy.
Daisy who?
Daisy goes to school, nights
  he sleeps!

Knock knock!
Who's there?
Philip.
Philip who?
Philip the tub, I need a bath!

Knock knock!
Who's there?
Ivana.
Ivana who?
Ivana go home!

Knock knock!
Who's there?
House.
House who?
House it going?

Knock knock!
Who's there?
Abbott.
Abbott who?
Ab-bott time you asked!

Knock knock!
Who's there?
Belize.
Belize who?
Belize let me in!

CLASSIC CARD GAME: GO FISH

*Go Fish is a fun, classic game of trying to steal the best cards
from your opponent's hand to complete pairs in your own.*

This game requires two to six players, playing with
a standard pack of fifty-two cards.

OBJECTIVE:

To reel in the most matching pairs of cards, while helping to develop pairing and matching skills.

1. A random dealer is selected, who deals six cards face down to each
   player. The remaining cards are placed face down in the center of the
   table. Play begins with all players laying down any pair(s) of cards that
   they have in their hand. Then the dealer is first to act. He gets to ask
   another player for a card of a specific value in the hopes of making a
   pair with a card in his hand.

2. If the player has that card he must give it to the person who asked,
   and he places that card with the matching card in his hand and lays
   them down. He may then ask another player for a card. Anytime a player
   does not have the card that he's asked for, he says, "Go Fish," and the
   player who asked takes a card out of the pool on the table. If the card
   picked up is the card asked for (a catch), he places the pair down and
   may ask another player for a card. If it is not the card asked for, his turn
   ends and it is the next player's turn. Play continues in the same fashion
   around the table until one player's hand is gone or the pool is drained.
   The player with the most pairs wins the game.

3. *Variations:* In one variation, a player must collect all four cards (a "book") before laying them down. Therefore, in play, you will ask another player for all of the suits of the card that you want (that is, "Give me all of your threes"). Instead of taking cards out of the pool, you can play with a stockpile, and if the player has to go fish, he takes the top card. In the variation called Authors, players must ask for a specific card including its suit—"Give me the queen of hearts" instead of "Give me your queens."

"*A two-year-old is kind of like having a blender, but you don't have a top for it.*"

—JERRY SEINFELD

The Brave Tin Soldier

ADAPTED FROM THE STORY BY HANS CHRISTIAN ANDERSEN

O NCE UPON A TIME there was a little tin soldier made from an old spoon. He was one of twenty-five soldiers made from the same tin spoon. They all stood straight and wore decorated uniforms of red and blue. They were all exactly alike, except for one who had only one leg. He had been the last one made and there had not been enough tin to finish him.

The little boy who was given the twenty-five soldiers loved his one-legged tin soldier best of all. On the table where the boy played with his tin soldiers was a small black puzzle box, and a beautiful white-paper ballerina who held a red rose made of tinsel and glitter in her hands. Her dress was made from a fine silk handkerchief.

As soon as the tin soldier glimpsed her across the table, he fell in love. "She stands as straight and true as a soldier. I would give anything in the world to be with her."

Just then, a little mischief making goblin, who lived in the black puzzle box, popped out and said, "Tin Soldier, stop wishing for things you cannot have."

The tin soldier ignored the goblin. He was fascinated by the ballerina, who stood high on one tiptoe with her other leg stretched out. They both stood on one leg, so they had that in common, the tin soldier thought to himself.

The goblin was jealous of the attention that the tin soldier was giving to the ballerina, so he pushed the tin soldier off the table and out the window!

The little tin soldier fell to the ground, where he was found by two little boys.

"Look, there's a tin soldier!" said one boy.

"Let's put him in a boat," said the other boy.

So they built a small boat and set the tin soldier afloat. Down the tiny stream he floated, standing straight and still.

At the entrance to the sewer stood a rat.

"Halt! Who goes there?" demanded the rat.

The tin soldier said nothing and floated past the ranting rat into the dark sewer where he swirled around in the darkness and floated out into the great river.

It wasn't long before a fish in the river saw the glint from the soldier's red coat and snapped him up in one bite. A moment later, the fish found itself caught in a net and hauled ashore.

"This is all the goblin's fault," thought the tin soldier. "If only the ballerina were here with me, I wouldn't mind being caught in this fish's belly."

Just then, there was a poke of a knife, and the fish's belly was slit open wide.

"Why look!" said the boy's mother, "here is the lost tin soldier!" The fish had been caught and taken to market, and sold to the family of the very boy who owned the tin soldier.

The mother cleaned the soldier and put him back on the table where all of his brothers welcomed him home with quiet salutes.

The tin soldier was pleased to be back at last in full sight of the ballerina whom he loved.

Perhaps it was the goblin's curse, or perhaps it was just a mistake, but at that moment the boy ran into the room in a rage. He was angry because he had been unable to find his favorite toy, a special set of colorful marbles.

He picked up the tin soldier, which was the first thing he saw, and threw him into the fireplace.

The tin soldier felt the heat of the flames melting first his hat and then his gun. His legs were turning as red as his coat, and soon he knew he would be melted and gone.

Suddenly, though, the door to the room flew open, and a gust of wind caught the little ballerina. She blew into the air, and landed in the fire right next to the tin soldier. For a moment they stood beside each other, engulfed in bright flames.

In the next instant the ballerina caught on fire, and was gone. The tin soldier melted down into a little tin lump.

The next morning, there was nothing left of the little tin soldier but a tiny tin lump, shaped like a heart. Of the little dancer, nothing was left but her tinsel and glitter rose.

I Saw a Ship A-Sailing

I saw a ship a-sailing,
A-sailing on the sea;
And, oh, it was all laden
With pretty, things for thee.

There were comfits in the cabin,
And apples in the hold;
The sails were made of silk,
And the masts were made of gold.

The four-and-twenty sailors
That stood between the decks,
Were four-and-twenty white mice
With chains about their necks.

The captain was a duck,
With a packet on his back;
And when the ship began to move,
The captain said, "Quack! Quack!"

"The only way I can describe [fatherhood]—it sounds stupid, but—at the end of How the Grinch Stole Christmas, *you know how his heart grows like five times? Everything is full; it's just full all the time."*

—MATT DAMON

CLASSIC CARD GAME: OLD MAID

Nobody wants to be the Old Maid! That's the mission of this game. A traditional Old Maid card deck contains matching cards of various occupations. The Old Maid card is the elderly, single woman without a matching card.

Old Maid requires two or more players and helps to develop matching and pairing skills. You'll want to use a special Old Maid deck of cards, or a standard pack of fifty-two cards minus one of the queens.

OBJECTIVE:

To get rid of all of your cards so that you're not the last player stuck with the Old Maid card.

1. A random dealer is selected and deals all of the cards out clockwise around the table. Players then discard any pairs that they have in their hand.
2. The dealer then begins play by offering his cards face down to the player on his left. That player may choose any of the cards displayed and add it to her hand. If this card makes a pair with any other card in her hand, she discards that pair. She then offers her cards to the player on her left. You are safe and out of the game once you have discarded all of the cards in your hand.
3. Play continues until only one player is left holding the Old Maid card (or the last queen). That player becomes the Old Maid and loses the game.

The Happy Prince

ADAPTED FROM THE STORY BY OSCAR WILDE

ONCE UPON A TIME, high above a city on a tall column stood the statue of the Happy Prince. He was gilded all over and had two bright sapphire eyes. His sword hilt was decorated with a sparkling ruby.

He was very much admired, indeed. "He is as beautiful as a weathervane," remarked one of the town council members who wished to gain a reputation for having artistic tastes.

"Why can't you be like the Happy Prince?" asked a sensible mother of her little boy who was crying for a toy he couldn't have. "The Happy Prince never dreams of crying for anything."

One night there flew over the city a little bird, a swallow. His friends had all flown to Egypt for the winter, but he had stayed behind. He saw the statue on the tall column and decided to rest there for the night. So he landed there just between the feet of the Happy Prince.

Just as he was putting his head under his wing to sleep, a large drop of water fell on him. "How strange!" he cried, "there is not a single cloud in the sky."

Then another drop fell.

"What is the use of a statue if it cannot keep the rain off?" he said. "I must look for a good chimney," and he decided to fly away. But before he had opened his wings, a third drop fell, and he looked up, and saw— and what did he see? The eyes of the Happy Prince were filled with tears, and tears were running down his golden cheeks. His face was so beautiful in the moonlight that the little swallow was filled with pity.

"Who are you?" he asked.

"I am the Happy Prince."

"Why are you crying then?" asked the swallow.

"When I was alive and had a human heart," answered the statue, "I did not know what tears were, because I lived in the palace of Sans-Souci, where sorrow is not allowed. I was called the Happy Prince, and happy indeed I was, if you think pleasure is happiness. Now that I am dead, they have set me up here so high that I can see all the ugliness and misery of my city. And though my heart is made of lead I can't help but cry.

"Far away," continued the statue, "there is a poor house. One of the windows is open, and through it I can see a woman seated at a table. Her face is thin and worn, and she has coarse, red hands, all pricked by the needle, for she is a seamstress. In a bed in the corner of the room, her little boy is lying ill. He has a fever and is asking for oranges. His mother has nothing to give him but river water, so he is crying. Swallow, will you not bring her the ruby out of my sword-hilt since I can't move?"

"My friends are waiting for me in Egypt," said the swallow.

"Swallow," said the prince, "the boy is so thirsty, and the mother so sad."

"I don't think I like boys," answered the swallow. "Last summer, when I was staying on the river, there were two rude boys, the miller's sons, who were always throwing stones at me."

The Happy Prince looked so sad that the little swallow was sorry. "It is very cold here," he said, "but I will stay with you for one night, and be your messenger."

"Thank you, little swallow," said the prince.

So the swallow picked out the great ruby from the prince's sword and flew away with it in his beak. At last he came to the poor house and looked in. The boy was tossing feverishly on his bed, and the mother had fallen asleep. In he hopped and laid the great ruby on the table beside the woman's thimble. Then he flew gently round the bed, fanning the boy's forehead with his wings.

"How cool I feel," said the boy, "I must be getting better."

Then the swallow flew back to the Happy Prince and told him what he had done. "It is strange," he remarked, "but I feel quite warm now, even though it's so cold."

"That is because you have done a good deed," said the prince.

"Tonight I go to Egypt," said the swallow, and he was happy at the thought. The sparrow explored the city and when the moon rose he flew back to the Happy Prince. "I am getting ready to go to Egypt," he told the prince.

"Swallow," asked the prince, "will you please stay one more night?"

"My friends are waiting for me in Egypt," answered the swallow.

"Swallow," said the prince, "far away across the city I see a young man in an attic. He is leaning over a desk covered with papers. He is trying to finish a play for the theater, but he is too cold to write any more. There is no fire in the grate."

"I will stay one more night," said the swallow, who really had a good heart. "Shall I take him another ruby?"

"Unfortunately, I have no ruby now," said the prince. "My eyes are all that I have left. They are made of rare sapphires, which were brought out of India a thousand years ago. Pluck out one of them and take it to him. He will sell it to the jeweler, and buy food and firewood, and finish his play."

"Dear Prince," said the Swallow, "I can't do that," and he began to cry.

"Swallow," said the prince, "do as I ask of you."

So the swallow plucked out the prince's eye and flew away to the student's attic. It was easy enough to get in, as there was a hole in the roof. Through this he darted and came into the room. The young man had his head buried in his hands, so he did not hear the flutter of the bird's wings, and when he looked up he found the beautiful sapphire.

"This must be from some great admirer. Now I can finish my play," he said, and he looked quite happy.

When the moon rose the next day, the swallow came to bid the prince good-bye.

"Swallow," said the prince, "please stay one more night."

"Dear Prince," said the swallow, "I must leave you. But I will never forget you, and next spring I will bring you back two beautiful jewels in place of those you have given away. The ruby shall be redder than a red rose, and the sapphire shall be as blue as the great sea."

"In the square below," said the Happy Prince, "there stands a little match-girl. She has let her matches fall in the gutter, and they are all spoiled. Her father will beat her if she does not bring home some money, and she is crying. She has no shoes or stockings, and her little head is bare. Pluck out my other eye, and give it to her, and her father will not beat her."

"I will stay with you one night longer," said the swallow, "but I cannot pluck out your eye. You would be blind then."

"Swallow," said the Prince, "do as I ask."

So he plucked out the prince's other eye and darted down with it. He swooped past the match-girl, and slipped the jewel into the palm of her hand. "What a lovely bit of glass," cried the little girl, and she ran home, laughing.

Then the swallow came back to the prince. "You are blind now," he said, "so I will stay with you always."

"No, little swallow," said the poor Prince, "you must go away to Egypt."

"No, I will stay with you always," said the swallow, and he slept at the prince's feet.

All the next day he sat on the prince's shoulder and told him stories of what he had seen in strange lands.

"Dear little swallow," said the prince, "you tell me of marvelous things, but more important than anything is the sadness of men and of women. Fly over my city, little swallow, and tell me what you see there."

So the swallow flew over the great city and saw the rich making merry in their beautiful houses, while the beggars were sitting at the gates.

Then he flew back and told the prince what he had seen.

"I am covered with fine gold," said the prince, "you must take it off, piece by piece, and give it to my poor. The living always think that gold can make them happy."

The swallow picked off the gold, till the Happy Prince looked quite dull and gray. He brought leaf after leaf of the fine gold to the poor. The children's faces grew rosier, and they laughed and played games in the street.

Then the snow came, and after the snow came the frost. The streets looked as if they were made of silver, they were so bright and glistening.

The poor little swallow grew colder and colder, but he would not leave the prince; he loved him so much. He picked up crumbs outside the baker's door when the baker was not looking and tried to keep himself warm by flapping his wings.

But at last he knew that he was going to die. He had just strength to fly up to the prince's shoulder once more.

"Goodbye, dear Prince!" he murmured.

"I am glad that you are going to Egypt at last, little swallow," said the prince, "you have stayed too long here. But you must kiss me on the lips, for I love you."

"It is not to Egypt that I am going," said the swallow. "I am dying."

And he kissed the Happy Prince on the lips and fell down dead at his feet.

At that moment a curious crack sounded inside the statue, as if something had broken. The fact is that the leaden heart had snapped right in two. It certainly was a dreadfully hard frost.

Early the next morning the mayor was walking in the square below with the town council members. As they passed the column he looked up at the statue: "How shabby the Happy Prince looks!" he said.

"The ruby has fallen out of his sword, his eyes are gone, and he isn't gold anymore," said the mayor. "In fact, he is little better than a beggar!"

"And, to make things worse, there is actually a dead bird at his feet!" continued the mayor.

So they pulled down the statue of the Happy Prince.

"As he is no longer beautiful, he is no longer useful," said the art professor at the university.

Then they melted the statue in a furnace, and the mayor held a meeting of the corporation to decide what was to be done with the metal. "We must have another statue, of course," he said, "and it shall be a statue of myself."

"Of myself!" cried each of the town council members and they quarreled. In fact, they are quarreling still.

The statue was dismantled and sent to be melted down, but the prince's broken lead heart would not melt. It was tossed into the garbage, where it landed next to the poor, dead swallow. Now, both are in paradise where they continue their good deeds.

BASEBALL TERMS TO KNOW

When you watch sports games with your kids, they might want to know what certain terms mean so they can follow along. Here's a glossary of key baseball words.

CATCHER The catcher crouches behind home plate to catch any pitches that the batter doesn't hit. If a runner tries to steal a base, the catcher tries to throw the runner out.

CHOKING UP Sometimes a coach will suggest that you choke up on the bat. This means to hold your hands higher above the end of the bat. Choking up makes it easier to contact the ball, but more difficult to hit the ball hard.

FIELDING PERCENTAGE One measure of a fielder's strength is the fielding percentage. To calculate this stat, add the player's putouts and assists. Then, divide by the total of the player's putouts, assists, and errors. A good fielder will have a fielding percentage of .980 or .990. Outfielders are expected to have higher fielding percentages than infielders.

FLY OUT If a fielder catches a batted ball before it hits the ground, the batter is out.

GROUND OUT If a fielder throws the ball to first base before the batter gets there, the batter is out.

INNING A turn at bat for each team is called an inning. A professional or college baseball game lasts for nine innings. High school and Little League games are usually shorter—five, six, or seven innings.

INFIELDERS Those who play first base, second base, third base, and shortstop are called infielders. Infielders play close to the batter and to the bases. They field ground balls and try to throw the batter out. When a ball is hit into the outfield, the infielders receive the ball from the outfielders and try to tag out runners.

NO-HITTER When a pitcher allows no hits in a game, it's called a no-hitter. It's still a no-hitter if the pitcher walks batters or if batters reach base on fielding errors. In fact, it's possible for a pitcher to pitch a no-hitter but still lose the game!

OUTFIELDERS The right fielder, left fielder, and center fielder are the outfielders. They play far away from the batter and the bases. Their main job is to catch fly balls and to throw the ball back to the infielders.

PITCHER The pitcher starts all the action on the field by throwing every pitch to the batter. Pitchers also have to field ground balls and help out the infielders.

PULL HITTER A right-handed pull hitter tends to hit the ball to left field every time. (Of course, a left-handed pull hitter tends to hit to right field.) Pull hitters usually generate a lot of power, but they are easy to defend against. The best hitters can also hit to the opposite field—in other words, a right-handed hitter will be able to hit toward right field.

STRIKEOUT A batter gets a strike if he swings and misses, or if he doesn't swing at a good pitch. Three strikes and the batter is out.

TAGGED OUT If a runner is not touching a base and is tagged with the ball, the runner is out.

UMPIRE Umpires referee baseball games. They decide all close calls. Is the pitch a ball or a strike? Is the runner safe or out? Is the ball fair or foul? The umpire's decision is final. A good umpire can make a game much more fun: Since the ump makes all the close decisions, instead of arguing with the other team, you can spend your time playing the game.

"I cannot think of any need in childhood as strong as the need for a father's protection."

—SIGMUND FREUD

When Papa Comes Home

You shall have an apple,
You shall have a plum,
You shall have a rattle-basket,
When papa comes home.

Rub-A-Dub-Dub

Rub-a-dub-dub
Three men in a tub,
And how do you think they got there?
The butcher, the baker, the candlestick maker,
They all jumped out of a rotten potato,
'Twas enough to make a man stare.

HOW TO MAKE YOUR OWN FOSSILS

*You and your little archaeologist will love searching for differ-
ent items to make fossil prints with. Let your creativity run wild
as you dig in and make your very own unique fossils!*

WHAT YOU'LL NEED:

½ cup flour

½ cup used coffee grounds

¼ cup salt

¼ cup sand

Water

Fossil objects such as: sea shells, leaves, feathers, toy dinosaurs, rocks,
pine needles, ferns/foliage, cleaned bones (left over from chicken or meat)

1. Mix together all of the dry ingredients.
2. Add the water a little at a time until you have a thick dough-like consistency.
3. Flatten the dough to about 1" thick, and break the dough into the desired sizes.
4. Choose the objects you want to make into fossils and carefully press them into the dough.
5. Let your fossil dry completely before you share or display your findings!

ALL-TIME FOOTBALL GREATS

Football is the most popular sport in America—so if you and your kids are watching it, why not learn about some of history's greatest players and coaches?

PAUL BROWN

Paul Brown was perhaps the best football coach ever. He won state championships at Massillon High School in Ohio. Later, he won national championships with the Ohio State Buckeyes. So when he was appointed as the first head coach of the AAFC's Cleveland Browns, he was already famous.

RED GRANGE

The Galloping Ghost first became nationally famous while he played for the University of Illinois. In a 1924 game at Michigan, he scored five touchdowns, four of which came in the first quarter. Red joined the Chicago Bears after graduation, where he earned the then-unimaginable salary of $100,000 for the season.

DARRELL GREEN

In 1983, the Washington Redskins chose cornerback Darrell Green in the first round. He played for the Redskins for twenty years. In three championship games, Darrell caught an interception and scored a touchdown on a punt return. Darrell's presence could not only shut down a receiver on his side of the field, but he could force the offense to run to the other side of the field, too.

JOE NAMATH

Jets quarterback Joe Namath guaranteed his team would win Super Bowl III, even though the Colts were heavily favored. Namath proved the media and the analysts wrong and earned the MVP award in the game. He was one of professional football's first superstars, appearing in movies and TV shows.

EMMITT SMITH

Running back Emmitt Smith is best known for his thirteen years with the Dallas Cowboys, during which he helped lead the team to three Super Bowl victories. Because Emmitt was so successful in the pros, many fans forget his outstanding career at the University of Florida, which earned him a place in the College Football Hall of Fame.

JOE MONTANA

Joe Cool, as he became known, started his career with the San Francisco 49ers in 1979. In only his third year, he led the 49ers to their best NFL season ever: a 13-3 record and a playoff berth. Joe was named the most valuable player in three of his four Super Bowl victories. Throughout his career, Joe was known for his grace under pressure. Twenty-six times he led the 49ers to come-from-behind wins.

WALTER PAYTON

Walter "Sweetness" Payton played in the NFL for thirteen years, from 1975–1987. In 1975, the Chicago Bears drafted him with their first pick. Walter set eight NFL records in his career, including the most rushing yards in a single game, most career rushing yards, and most career total yards. Walter Payton remains perhaps the most loved Bear in recent history.

JERRY RICE

Jerry Rice played for sixteen years with the 49ers and another three years with the Raiders and Seahawks. He was the greatest receiver ever to play. He led the league six times in receiving yards and touchdown receptions, retiring with the most receiving yardage of anyone in NFL history. Jerry played in four Super Bowls—three with the 49ers and one with the Raiders—and he caught a touchdown in each one and was named Super Bowl XXIII MVP.

BARRY SANDERS

Barry played running back for the Detroit Lions for ten seasons, from 1989–1998. He led the NFL in rushing four times and went to the Pro Bowl every single season. Barry didn't bowl over the defense—rather, he spun and juked and left defenders grabbing at air as he whooshed by.

JIM THORPE

Jim Thorpe was the best football player in the early days of the NFL and the best all-around athlete of the twentieth century. He was best known for his amazing track and field performances in the 1912 Olympics. Later, he played major league baseball as well as professional football.

GLENN SCOBEY "POP" WARNER

Pop Warner was a standout football player at Cornell University who went on to coach college football for forty-five years, starting in 1895. He is the one who had the idea for players to wear numbers, and he also introduced the huddle, screen pass, and many other football techniques. He supported a youth football league in Philadelphia in the 1930s. The league eventually became the Pop Warner Conference.

REGGIE WHITE

Reggie, a defensive end nicknamed The Minister of Defense, was an All-American player for the University of Tennessee. His NFL career included dominant years with both the Philadelphia Eagles and the Green Bay Packers. He won the NFL Defensive Player of the Year twice, was a 13-time Pro Bowl selection, and holds second place all-time among career sack leaders with 198.5.

JUST FOR LAUGHS

What did one casket say to the other casket?
"Is that you coffin?"

What do basketball players get?
Hooping cough.

How do you spell "mousetrap" with only three letters?
C-A-T.

What color is a kitten's meow?
Purr-ple.

Luna: I must be sick. I'm see-ing spots.
Larry: Have you seen a doctor?
Luna: No, just spots.

Alex: Teacher! Teacher! Jimmy just swallowed four quarters!
Teacher: Now, why would he do that?
Alex: It's his lunch money.

If we breathe oxygen during the day, what do we breathe at night?
Nitrogen.

What's the hottest day of the week?
Fry day.

What is at the center of Jupiter?
The letter "I."

What do you call a chubby dog?
A round hound.

A full-grown stegosaurus can grow up to how many feet?
Just the four.

What has 18 legs, spits, and catches flies?
A baseball team.

Rosie: Do you think my painting is any good?
Bill: In a way.
Rosie: What kind of way?
Bill: Away off.

There was a young lady named Bright
Whose speed was much faster than light.
She went out one day
In a relative way
And came back on the previous night.

"This report card should be underwater!"

"Because it's so wet?"

"No, because it's below 'C' level!"

"What are you having for dinner tonight?"

"Reruns."

"Reruns?"

"Yeah, leftover TV dinners."

Where's the best place to find cows?

At a moo-see-'em.

How many wizards does it take to change a light bulb? Depends on what you want the light bulb to change into.

Rip Van Winkle

ADAPTED FROM THE STORY BY WASHINGTON IRVING

ONCE UPON A TIME, high in the Catskill Mountains, lived an amiable fellow named Rip Van Winkle. Rip Van Winkle was not an ambitious guy; and in fact some, including his wife, called him lazy.

He was, though, a very popular fellow who, as far as anyone could tell, had just one failing: his uncanny ability to find employment and business anywhere but on his own farm. He could fish all day without a single nibble. The women of the village asked him to run their errands and to do other odd jobs since their own husbands wouldn't. In short, Rip took care of everyone's business except his own!

Rip Van Winkle was happy and would have believed his life to be quite perfect if it weren't for one particularly pesky thorn in his side: his wife. She kept at him day and night about his chronic idleness, his carelessness, and the ruin he was bringing on his family.

Rip's only friend at home was his dog, Wolf. As frequently as possible, both Rip and Wolf would sneak out of the house and sit on the bench outside the town's inn, underneath the sign with the picture of His Majesty George the Third. There they would sit and talk with other lazy folk like Derrick Van Bummel, the schoolmaster, or Nicholas Vedder, the landlord of the inn.

One fine autumn day, Rip put his musket on his shoulder, whistled Wolf to his side, and climbed up to one of the highest points of the

Catskill Mountains. He hunted squirrel for a bit. Then, panting and fatigued, he threw himself on a green knoll and snoozed in peace.

"Rip Van Winkle!" said a voice. And he woke with a start. Was that his wife calling him all this way? Surely it was only his imagination; still it was time to be on his way. He stood up and was about to head back into the village, when he heard the voice again. "Rip Van Winkle! Rip Van Winkle!"

He looked round and saw nothing but a crow. At the same time, though, Wolf bristled up his back and gave a low growl. Then Rip saw a strange, short, square-built man lumbering toward him. He had thick bushy hair and a grizzled beard. Rip followed the short fellow up into the mountains, wondering where it was they might be going.

As they climbed, Rip heard sounds like distant thunder that seemed to come from a deep ravine. Here, the short man poured a glass of liquid from his keg for Rip, who obliged by taking a small taste. One sip led to another, and soon he had drunk the whole glass. Now, his eyes swam in his head, his head gradually declined, and he fell into a deep sleep.

On waking, he found himself on the green knoll where he had first seen the old man. He rubbed his eyes—it was a bright sunny morning. "Surely," thought Rip, "I have not slept here all night." He recalled the occurrences before he fell asleep—the strange man with a keg of potent liquid, the mountain ravine, and the deep sleep. For now, though, he was worried about what his wife would have to say about his absence!

He looked round for his gun, but in place of the clean, well-oiled musket, he found an old gun lying by him, the barrel coated with rust, the lock falling off, and the stock filled with worm holes. Perhaps that fellow had played a trick on him, poisoning his drink and taking his gun. Wolf, too, had disappeared, but he might have strayed away after a squirrel or partridge. Rip whistled and shouted, but with no success.

As he rose to walk, he found himself stiff in the joints. He again called and whistled for his dog; he was answered only by the cawing of a flock of idle crows. He shook his head, shouldered the rusty musket, and, with a heart full of trouble and worry, turned his steps homeward.

As he approached the village, he met a number of people, but he didn't recognize any of them. This somewhat surprised him, for he had thought himself acquainted with everyone in the area.

Their clothing, too, seemed different. They all stared at him in surprise. The constant recurrence of this gesture caused Rip, involuntarily, to do the same, and, to his astonishment, he found his beard had grown over a foot long!

A cluster of children ran at his heels, hooting and hollering after him, and pointing at his long gray beard. He hardly recognized his village. It was larger and more crowded. There were rows of houses that he had never seen before. Strange names were over the doors, strange faces at the windows—everything was strange. What was going on? he wondered.

It was with some difficulty that he found the way to his own house, which he approached with reluctance, expecting every moment to hear the shrill voice of Mrs. Van Winkle. He found the house gone to ruin—the roof fallen in, the windows shattered, and the doors off their hinges. A half-starved dog that looked like Wolf was skulking about, but it only snarled at him.

The house appeared abandoned. He called loudly for his wife and children, but there was no response. He went to the village inn, but it too was gone. Instead he found a large hotel, and even its sign was strange. Gone was the ruby face of King George. The red coat was changed for one of blue, and the new fellow's head was decorated with a cocked hat. Underneath was painted in large characters, GENERAL WASHINGTON.

Eventually, a group of villagers gathered around this odd looking man. Rip thought for a moment, and then inquired of them, "Where's Nicholas Vedder?"

"Nicholas Vedder! Why, he's been dead for eighteen years!"

"Where's Brom Dutcher, or Van Bummel, the schoolmaster?"

"They went off to the army at the beginning of the war. Dutcher never came back. Van Bummel became a great general and is now in Congress."

Rip's heart sunk. At last he cried out in despair, "Does nobody here know Rip Van Winkle?"

"Oh, Rip Van Winkle!" exclaimed two or three, "Oh, yes! That's Rip Van Winkle up there, leaning against the tree."

Rip looked up and saw an exact image of himself as he looked the day he went up the mountain: apparently as lazy, and certainly as rough around the edges. The poor fellow was now completely mystified. He doubted his own identity and whether he was himself or another man.

"Who are you? What's your name?" asked the gathered crowd.

"I'm not sure," said the old fellow.

At this critical moment a familiar looking woman with a baby in her arms came to peek at Rip.

"What is your name, my good woman?" he asked.

"Judith Gardenier."

"And what was your father's name?"

"Oh, poor man. Rip Van Winkle was his name, but it's been twenty years since he went away from home with his gun and never has been heard of since—his dog came home without him. We don't know what happened to him."

Rip had only one more question to ask: "Where's your mother?"

"Oh, she too died. She died in a fit of rage!"

Well, at least this was good news, thought Rip.

Finally, Rip said, "I am your father. Young Rip Van Winkle once— old Rip Van Winkle now! Does nobody know poor Rip Van Winkle?"

All stood amazed, until an old woman, tottering out from among the crowd, put her hand to her brow, and peering under it at his face for a moment, exclaimed, "Sure enough! It is Rip Van Winkle—it is himself! Welcome home again, old neighbor. Why, where have you been these twenty years?"

Rip's story was soon told, for the whole twenty years had passed for him as just one night.

Rip's daughter took him home to live with her. She had a snug house, and a round, happy farmer for a husband, whom Rip remembered as one of the urchins who used to torment him. As for Rip's son and heir, who was lazy like Rip Senior, he attended to just about anything except his business.

For many years, Rip Van Winkle (Senior) could be found hanging out at the new village inn, under the sign of George Washington, recounting the story of his strange travels into the mountains. Often Rip Van Winkle (Junior) would find the time to be there, too!

BASKETBALL SKILL GAMES

H-O-R-S-E

Want to sharpen your basketball skills as a family? One classic game is H-O-R-S-E, a shot-making game of skill. You take a shot from anywhere on the court. If you make it, your opponent has to make a shot from the same place. If they miss, they get the letter H. Keep playing until one of you ends up with five letters—H-O-R-S-E—at which point that player has lost. You can do long shots, close shots, free throws, layups, and even trick shots.

AROUND THE WORLD

Around the World works best if you play it with one or two others. Start by making a layup, then backing up with two or three shots on the hash marks of the key. The hash marks denote where players stand during free throws, with the first spot reserved for the players from the defending team, and then alternating with offensive and defensive players. There are spots for four players on each side of the free throw area. To continue doing this drill, once you shoot a free throw, you go to the top of the key to make a three pointer before closing in toward the hoop again by making shots from the hash marks on the other side of the key. To finish, you make a layup.

TWENTY-ONE

The game is played to twenty-one points. You receive one point for a free throw, two points from inside the three-point line, and three points from behind the three-point line. You can play the game with two or more players. One player starts with the ball; the others position themselves to try to grab a rebound. The player with the ball shoots a free throw. If she makes it, she gets one point and gets the ball back for another free throw. If she makes the second free throw, she racks up another point and gets possession of the ball at the top of the key. She can make a shot from anywhere on the court, but now the other players can play defense. If she makes the shot, she earns more points and goes back to the free throw line to start the cycle again. If a player misses a free throw, the ball is considered live, and any player can rebound it. Whoever comes away with the ball has to dribble it past the three-point line before trying to make a shot. If he makes it, it's his turn to go to the free throw line. The first player to get twenty-one points is the winner.

Little Tom Tucker

Little Tom Tucker
Sings for his supper.
What shall he eat?
White bread and butter.
How will he cut it
Without ever a knife?
How will he be married
Without ever a wife?

Georgie Porgie

Georgie Porgie, pudding and pie,
Kissed the girls and made them cry.
When the boys came out to play,
Georgie Porgie ran away.

Little Boy Blue

Little Boy Blue, come, blow
your horn!
The sheep's in the meadow,
the cow's in the corn.
But where is the boy who
looks after the sheep?
He's under the haystack,
fast asleep!

HOW TO MAKE YOUR OWN CRAYONS

Tired of throwing away broken crayons? Here's a great way to recycle them!

WHAT YOU'LL NEED:
Broken crayon pieces
Mini muffin pan
Nonstick cooking spray

1. Preheat oven to 275°F. Coat the pan very lightly with nonstick cooking spray.

2. Remove any paper from the old crayons, and break them into small pieces. Fill the muffin tin with the crayon pieces. You can make multi-colored crayons, or group similar colors together, whatever you like!

3. Bake the crayons until they have melted, about 7–8 minutes. (Note: When the crayons begin to melt, you can use a toothpick to swirl and blend the colors.)

4. Remove the muffin pan from the oven, let your new crayons cool, and color away!

"When I was a boy of 14, my father was so ignorant I could hardly stand to have the old man around. But when I got to be 21, I was astonished at how much he had learned in 7 years."

—ATTRIBUTED TO MARK TWAIN

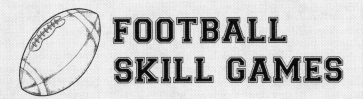

FOOTBALL SKILL GAMES

MAN-TO-MAN COVERAGE

The quarterback says "hike," and a receiver runs out for a pass. One defender tries to intercept or knock down the pass. The receiver gets one point for a complete pass, and the defender gets two points for an incomplete pass. Make a time limit of, say, three seconds for the quarterback to release the ball.

TARGET ACCURACY GAME

Set up a group of targets—long cones, chairs, or tree trunks work fine. Assign each target a point value, with closer or bigger targets worth less. Put a bunch of footballs in front of a quarterback. Someone says "Go!" and times thirty seconds. The quarterback tries to earn as many points as possible by hitting the targets with the ball. Everyone else races to return the thrown balls to the quarterback. Then it's someone else's turn. See who can get the most points in thirty seconds.

PASS PATTERN GAME

This one takes a few more people—try using three receivers and two defenders. The receivers go out for a pass, but they all have to start and stay on only one side of the field. The quarterback has to throw the ball within three seconds. The receiver is down right after catching the ball. Give the offense one point for each yard they get on a completion; give the defense twenty points for an incomplete. You can adjust the scoring depending on the size of the field and the skill of the defenders. The offense should be able to win since they outnumber the defense, but a clever and quick defense can do well.

7-ON-7

In a 7-on-7 drill, the offensive and defensive lines are removed so the team can focus just on the passing game. The defense plays with three linebackers and four defensive backs; the offense gets a center, five running backs or receivers, and a quarterback.

THE TIP DRILL

One of the defenders' favorite drills is called the tip drill. In one version, the coach throws a pass to a running receiver, who deliberately misses the catch and tips the ball in the air. The defenders have to catch the ball for an interception. If they can't catch the ball cleanly, they're taught to try to keep the ball in the air. Defenses love interceptions, and they can make an interception on every play of this drill.

Polly Wolly Doodle

Oh, I went down South
For to see my Sal
Sing Polly wolly doodle all the day
My Sal, she is A spunky gal
Sing Polly wolly doodle all the day

(Chorus:) Fare thee well, Fare thee well,
Fare thee well my fairy fay
For I'm going to Lou'siana For to see my Susyanna
Sing Polly wolly doodle all the day

Oh, my Sal, she is a maiden fair
Sing Polly wolly doodle all the day
With curly eyes and laughing hair
Sing Polly wolly doodle all the day

(Chorus)

Behind the barn, Down on my knees
Sing Polly wolly doodle all the day
I thought I heard A chicken sneeze
Sing Polly wolly doodle all the day

(Chorus)

He sneezed so hard with the whooping cough
Sing Polly wolly doodle all the day
He sneezed his head and the tail right off
Sing Polly wolly doodle all the day

(Chorus)

Oh, a grasshopper sittin' On a railroad track
Sing Polly wolly doodle all the day
A-pickin' his teeth
With a carpet tack
Sing Polly wolly doodle all the day

(Chorus)

Oh, I went to bed But it wasn't any use
Sing Polly wolly doodle all the day
My feet stuck out Like a chicken roost
Sing Polly wolly doodle all the day

(Chorus)

CLASSIC CARD GAME: WAR

War is a classic card game enjoyed by both kids and adults. It is an easy game to learn and helps to develop matching and value recognition skills.

War requires two players, and you'll need a standard pack of fifty-two cards.

OBJECTIVE:

You battle your opponent and hope that you beat her card as you try to collect the entire deck.

1. A random dealer is selected, and he shuffles the cards. He then deals out the cards, one at a time, face down to each player. You both will have twenty-six cards that you keep face down in a neat pile in front of you.

2. Play begins with both of you turning over your top card. Speed is not a factor in this game, so there's no need to flip over your card quickly. The player who has the highest-ranking card gets to keep both cards. He turns those cards over and puts them face down at the bottom of his stack. You both then turn up your next card. Again, the player who has the highest card gets to take both cards. An ace takes a king, and a queen takes a six, and so on. The stacks will continue to grow, shrink, and grow again.

3. When you both turn up cards with an equal value, it's time for a war to break the tie. You'll each lay three cards face down and a final card face up. Whoever has the highest tiebreaker card wins the hand and claims the spoils of war—all eight cards. If the tiebreaker cards are of equal value, you'll have another battle and continue to do so until there are two different cards, and one player wins all of those cards.

4. The player who collects the entire deck wins the game. In order to win the game, you have to get the aces. Since aces are the highest cards, a lower card cannot beat it in a battle one on one. If you don't have an ace, you'll have to win one in an all-out war.

5. *Variation:* War can also be played with three or four players. The entire deck is dealt out, and during play the high card takes the other cards. When two cards match in a value, war breaks out, and all players participate—not just the two players with matching cards.

ALL-TIME BASEBALL GREATS

Baseball: It's America's pastime. Fathers have been telling their children about baseball's best hitters, fielders, and pitchers for generations—fulfill *your* fatherly duties and share these players' stories with your kids.

HANK AARON

Hank Aaron, nicknamed "the Hammer," played briefly in the Negro Leagues before being signed in 1954 by the Milwaukee Braves, who moved to Atlanta in 1966. Aaron belted at least 25 home runs 18 times, with a high of 47. He also posted more than 120 RBIs seven times while setting the all-time career RBI record. By the time he finished his 23-year career back in Milwaukee as a member of the Brewers, he was also near the top in games played, hits, runs scored, and doubles.

JOHNNY BENCH

There was never a greater major-league catcher than Johnny Bench. He broke into the major leagues when he was just 20 years old, making the All-Star Game and winning Rookie of the Year honors. In 1970, his third season, Bench won the National League MVP with 45 homers and 148 RBIs while leading the Reds to the World Series. Bench topped the 100 RBI mark on five occasions and was the main cog in Cincinnati's "Big Red Machine." Bench was also an incredible defensive catcher and was known for his great throwing arm. He won 10 Gold Glove

Awards. Two World Championships and consistently good play made Johnny Bench one of baseball's most popular players of the 1970s.

GEORGE BRETT

George Brett spent his entire career with the Royals, and that career coincided with the best years of the Kansas City Royals franchise. He was a .300 hitter who also hit 15–20 home runs every year. As if that weren't good enough, he was even better in the postseason. In the 1977 American League Championship Series (ALCS), he hit three home runs in the same game.

ROBERTO CLEMENTE

Roberto Clemente was a tremendous all-around ballplayer. Not only could he hit for a high average, but he had power and was a super defensive outfielder, winning 12 Gold Gloves. He joined the Pittsburgh Pirates in the mid-1950s as a 20-year-old rookie from Puerto Rico. He went on to become the greatest player from Puerto Rico and the first Hispanic player elected to the Hall of Fame. Clemente led the National League in batting four times in the 1960s, and four times he had more than 200 hits in a season. He appeared in two World Series for the Pirates and batted .362 overall, helping lead the Pirates to the title in 1971.

TY COBB

Ty Cobb was one of the best hitters ever. He recommended that hitters not hold the bat all the way at the bottom. He suggested holding the hands 1" from the knob and keeping the hands 1" apart from each other for better balance and bat control. Not everyone should hit this way, but Ty Cobb had a career .367 batting average and made the Hall of Fame, so his advice might work for your kids!

LOU GEHRIG

Gehrig was called the "Iron Horse" because he was always in the lineup and was as awesome a hitter as anyone. For 14 consecutive years he drove in more than 100 runs, topping 170 three times. He hit 40 home runs five times, and batted over .300 for 13 consecutive years. His 23 grand slam home runs is the all-time high. Unfortunately, Gehrig is best remembered for the reason he removed himself from the lineup eight games into the 1939 season. Gehrig had been suffering from an unknown disease, which later became known as Lou Gehrig's disease (ALS). He retired from baseball in May 1939, and in July he famously described himself as the "luckiest man on earth" for the opportunity to have played for the Yankees, and to have been loved by the fans and by his wife. Less than two years later he died at the age of 37.

KEN GRIFFEY JR.

For a long time, people just called him "Junior," because his dad was also named Ken Griffey and was a great player for the Cincinnati Reds and, briefly, the Seattle Mariners. He was one of the greatest center fielders ever, making many amazing catches and winning the Gold Glove for defense 10 years in a row. He was a major home run threat as well. Griffey hit his 500th home run in 2004, and he ended up fifth on the all-time home run list.

TONY GWYNN

From the moment he came up to the big leagues, Gwynn was the best hitter in baseball and one of the best of all time. His career .338 average is up there with the greats of the early 1900s. Gwynn led the league in batting seven times. He could hit any pitch for a single or double and hardly ever struck out, which helps explain why he had over 3,000 career hits. In his younger years he was also a great base stealer and tremendous defensive player. Gwynn retired at the end of the 2001 season after 20 years with the San Diego Padres and 19 consecutive .300 seasons.

WILLIE MAYS

He was known as the "Say Hey Kid" and was one of the greatest and most likable players to ever play the game. After his rookie season in 1951, Mays spent two years in the army before returning to the (then New York) Giants, with whom he racked up 41 homers and won the World Championship over the Cleveland Indians. He had great speed and was known for incredible defense too; with his basket catch, he used the glove as a "basket" to catch fly balls at his waist. Perhaps the most famous catch Mays ever made came in the first game of the 1954 World Series as he grabbed a ball going over his head to help the Giants hold on and win. Mays spent his last couple of years back in New York with the Mets before retiring as the third-greatest home run hitter ever.

REGGIE JACKSON

Reggie Jackson earned the nickname "Mr. October" because he was awesome when it was World Series time (in October). A great power hitter even in his rookie year in 1967, Jackson helped the Oakland A's win three consecutive World Series championships in 1972, 1973, and 1974. He later joined the Yankees and helped lead them to the World Series three times and to win two more World Championships. Reggie struck out a lot and wasn't a great defensive star, but when it was an important game, he was at his best. In Game 6 of the 1977 World Series, Jackson had what many consider the single best World Series game of any hitter ever. He hit three tremendous home runs and drove in five runs in the game.

CAL RIPKEN JR.

Cal Ripken Jr. was named Rookie of the Year in 1982 and MVP in 1983 and 1991. Ripken always came to play—and play hard—day in and day out. In late 1995, he went from a star to a legend when he broke a record that most thought could never be topped. Ripken played in his 2,131st consecutive game, breaking the iron horse record set by the great Lou Gehrig. Ripken played another 501 more consecutive games before taking himself out of the lineup in September 1998. During the 2001 season, Ripken announced his retirement after 20 years with the Baltimore Orioles. He was one of the best-liked and most respected individuals who ever played in the major leagues.

MIKE SCHMIDT

Many baseball fans consider Mike Schmidt to be the best all-around third baseman ever. He was a truly awesome power hitter, leading the league eight times in home runs. In just 17 years he placed himself among the top ten all-time leaders in homers, won three MVPs, and helped lead the Philadelphia Phillies to their first ever World Championship. He also won the Gold Glove as the best-fielding third baseman in the National League nine times. Fans and players alike respected and admired his talent and his work ethic.

TOM SEAVER

When "Tom Terrific" came up with the New York Mets in 1967, the Mets were the worst team in the major leagues. By 1969, they shocked everyone and won 100 games, with Tom Seaver winning 25 of them on the way to a World Championship. Seaver won his first of three Cy Young Awards that year and became the heart and soul of the Mets. Much to the disappointment of Mets fans, he was traded away in 1977, returning only for a brief stint before his retirement in 1986. In his career, he won 20 or more games four times and led the league in strikeouts five times. Seaver retired but returned to the Mets one more time—as an announcer.

OZZIE SMITH

Smith, a shortstop, was called the "Wizard of Oz" because he could get to groundballs that no one else could reach, often diving in either direction before somehow making the throw to first base for the out. He also turned more double plays than any player in history. Ozzie dazzled the fans and frustrated the opponents who thought they had a hit until he turned it into an out. He won a record 13 Gold Gloves and led the league nine times in fielding percentage at shortstop. He could also steal bases, picking up 580 in his 19-year career—that's more than 30 per year. Smith was a team leader and a fan favorite.

BABE RUTH

Nicknamed the Bambino, George Herman "Babe" Ruth could do it all. He began as a pitcher with the Boston Red Sox before moving to the outfield. He was traded to the Yankees, where he became the greatest home run hitter ever. Ruth's 714 home runs stood as the record until Hank Aaron passed that mark in 1974. He also batted .342 for his career and is still considered by most baseball historians as the greatest baseball player ever. Ruth led the Yankees to one World Series title after another. An often-told story says that in one World Series game against the Cubs, Ruth stepped up to the plate, pointed to the bleachers where he was going to hit a home run . . . and then did just that.

NOLAN RYAN

Nolan Ryan was truly a flame-thrower, firing the ball harder and faster than anyone had ever seen. When Ryan came up with the Mets in 1966 he could throw very hard, but he had control problems and walked a lot of hitters. In 1972, the Mets traded him to the California Angels, and there he turned into a big winner and became the king of strikeouts. In 1973 he struck out a whopping 383 hitters. While most pitchers would be thrilled to throw one no-hitter in their careers, Ryan threw seven— a major-league record. Ryan surprised everyone by pitching in the big leagues until he retired at age 46. By that time he had over 5,000 strike-outs, far more than anyone else.

TED WILLIAMS

Ted Williams, known as "The Splendid Splinter," was one of the most remarkable hitters ever. He hit for power, for a high average, and rarely ever struck out. In fact, after his career he wrote a book called *The Science of Hitting*, which is still a terrific book. In 1942, Williams not only led the league in batting average again, but also led with 37 home runs and 137 runs batted in, winning the Triple Crown. Williams's career was inter-rupted twice, once when he was drafted into the Navy for World War II, and again when he volunteered to serve in the Korean War.

Tweedledum and Tweedledee

Tweedledum and Tweedledee
Resolved to have a battle,
For Tweedledum said Tweedledee
Had spoiled his nice new rattle.

Just then flew by a monstrous crow,
As big as a tar barrel,
Which frightened both the heroes so,
They quite forgot their quarrel.

Little Jack Horner

Little Jack Horner
Sat in the corner,
Eating a Christmas pie:
He put in his thumb,
And pulled out a plum,
And said, "What a good boy am I!"

Tom Thumb

BY THE GRIMM BROTHERS

A **POOR WOODMAN** sat in his cottage one night, smoking his pipe by the fireside, while his wife sat by his side spinning. "How lonely it is, wife," said he, as he puffed out a long curl of smoke, "for you and me to sit here by ourselves, without any children to play about and amuse us while other people seem so happy and merry with their children!" "What you say is very true," said the wife, sighing, and turning round her wheel; "how happy should I be if I had but one child! If it were ever so small—nay, if it were no bigger than my thumb—I should be very happy, and love it dearly." Now—odd as you may think it—it came to pass that this good woman's wish was fulfilled, just in the very way she had wished it; for, not long afterwards, she had a little boy, who was quite healthy and strong, but was not much bigger than my thumb. So they said, "Well, we cannot say we have not got what we wished for, and, little as he is, we will love him dearly." And they called him Thomas Thumb.

They gave him plenty of food, yet for all they could do he never grew bigger, but kept just the same size as he had been when he was born. Still, his eyes were sharp and sparkling, and he soon showed himself to be a clever little fellow, who always knew well what he was about.

One day, as the woodman was getting ready to go into the wood to cut fuel, he said, "I wish I had someone to bring the cart after me, for I want to make haste." "Oh, father," cried Tom, "I will take care of that;

the cart shall be in the wood by the time you want it." Then the woodman laughed, and said, "How can that be? you cannot reach up to the horse's bridle." "Never mind that, father," said Tom; "if my mother will only harness the horse, I will get into his ear and tell him which way to go." "Well," said the father, "we will try for once."

When the time came the mother harnessed the horse to the cart, and put Tom into his ear; and as he sat there the little man told the beast how to go, crying out, "Go on!" and "Stop!" as he wanted: and thus the horse went on just as well as if the woodman had driven it himself into the wood. It happened that as the horse was going a little too fast, and Tom was calling out, "Gently! gently!" two strangers came up. "What an odd thing that is!" said one: "there is a cart going along, and I hear a carter talking to the horse, but yet I can see no one." "That is queer, indeed," said the other; "let us follow the cart, and see where it goes." So they went on into the wood, till at last they came to the place where the woodman was. Then Tom Thumb, seeing his father, cried out, "See, father, here I am with the cart, all right and safe! now take me down!" So his father took hold of the horse with one hand, and with the other took his son out of the horse's ear, and put him down upon a straw, where he sat as merry as you please.

The two strangers were all this time looking on, and did not know what to say for wonder. At last one took the other aside, and said, "That little urchin will make our fortune, if we can get him, and carry him about from town to town as a show; we must buy him." So they went up to the woodman, and asked him what he would take for the little man. "He will be better off," said they, "with us than with you." "I won't sell him at all," said the father; "my own flesh and blood is dearer to me than all the silver and gold in the world." But Tom, hearing of the bargain they wanted to make, crept up his father's coat to his shoulder and whispered in his ear, "Take the money, father, and let them have me; I'll soon come back to you."

So the woodman at last said he would sell Tom to the strangers for a large piece of gold, and they paid the price. "Where would you like to sit?" said one of them. "Oh, put me on the rim of your hat; that will be a nice gallery for me; I can walk about there and see the country as we go along." So they did as he wished; and when Tom had taken leave of his father they took him away with them.

They journeyed on till it began to be dusky, and then the little man said, "Let me get down, I'm tired." So the man took off his hat, and put him down on a clod of earth, in a ploughed field by the side of the road. But Tom ran about amongst the furrows, and at last slipped into an old mouse-hole. "Good night, my masters!" said he, "I'm off! mind and look sharp after me the next time." Then they ran at once to the place, and poked the ends of their sticks into the mouse-hole, but all in vain; Tom only crawled farther and farther in; and at last it became quite dark, so that they were forced to go their way without their prize, as sulky as could be.

When Tom found they were gone, he came out of his hiding-place. "What dangerous walking it is," said he, "in this ploughed field! If I were to fall from one of these great clods, I should undoubtedly break my neck." At last, by good luck, he found a large empty snail-shell. "This is lucky," said he, "I can sleep here very well"; and in he crept.

Just as he was falling asleep, he heard two men passing by, chatting together; and one said to the other, "How can we rob that rich parson's house of his silver and gold?" "I'll tell you!" cried Tom. "What noise was that?" said the thief, frightened; "I'm sure I heard someone speak." They stood still listening, and Tom said, "Take me with you, and I'll soon show you how to get the parson's money." "But where are you?" said they. "Look about on the ground," answered he, "and listen where the sound comes from." At last the thieves found him out, and lifted him up in their hands. "You little urchin!" they said, "what can you do for us?" "Why, I can get between the iron window-bars of the parson's house, and throw you out whatever you want." "That's a good thought," said the thieves; "come along, we shall see what you can do."

When they came to the parson's house, Tom slipped through the window-bars into the room, and then called out as loud as he could bawl, "Will you have all that is here?" At this the thieves were frightened, and said, "Softly, softly! Speak low, that you may not awaken anybody." But Tom seemed as if he did not understand them, and bawled out again, "How much will you have? Shall I throw it all out?" Now the cook lay in the next room; and hearing a noise she raised herself up in her bed and listened. Meantime the thieves were frightened, and ran off a little way; but at last they plucked up their hearts, and said, "The little urchin is only trying to make fools of us." So they came back and whispered softly to him, saying, "Now let us have no more of your roguish jokes; but throw us out some of the money." Then Tom called out as loud as he could, "Very well! hold your hands! here it comes."

The cook heard this quite plain, so she sprang out of bed, and ran to open the door. The thieves ran off as if a wolf was at their tails: and the maid, having groped about and found nothing, went away for a light. By the time she came back, Tom had slipped off into the barn; and when she had looked about and searched every hole and corner, and found nobody, she went to bed, thinking she must have been dreaming with her eyes open.

The little man crawled about in the hayloft, and at last found a snug place to finish his night's rest in; so he laid himself down, meaning to sleep till daylight, and then find his way home to his father and mother. But alas! how woefully he was undone! what crosses and sorrows happen to us all in this world! The cook got up early, before daybreak, to feed the cows; and going straight to the hayloft, carried away a large bundle of hay, with the little man in the middle of it, fast asleep. He still, however, slept on, and did not awake till he found himself in the mouth of the cow; for the cook had put the hay into the cow's rick, and the cow had taken Tom up in a mouthful of it. "Good lack-a-day!" said he, "how came I to tumble into the mill?" But he soon found out where he really was; and was forced to have all his wits about him, that he might not get between the cow's teeth, and so be crushed to death. At last down he went into her stomach. "It is rather dark," said he; "they forgot to build windows in this room to let the sun in; a candle would be no bad thing."

Though he made the best of his bad luck, he did not like his quarters at all; and the worst of it was, that more and more hay was always coming down, and the space left for him became smaller and smaller. At last he cried out as loud as he could, "Don't bring me any more hay! Don't bring me any more hay!"

The maid happened to be just then milking the cow; and hearing someone speak, but seeing nobody, and yet being quite sure it was the same voice that she had heard in the night, she was so frightened that she fell off her stool, and overset the milk pail. As soon as she could pick herself up out of the dirt, she ran off as fast as she could to her master the parson, and said, "Sir, sir, the cow is talking!" But the parson said, "Woman, thou art surely mad!" However, he went with her into the cow-house, to try and see what was the matter.

Scarcely had they set foot on the threshold, when Tom called out, "Don't bring me any more hay!" Then the parson himself was frightened; and thinking the cow was surely bewitched, told his man to kill her on the spot. So the cow was killed, and cut up; and the stomach, in which Tom lay, was thrown out upon a dunghill.

Tom soon set himself to work to get out, which was not a very easy task; but at last, just as he had made room to get his head out, fresh ill-luck befell him. A hungry wolf sprang out, and swallowed up the whole stomach, with Tom in it, at one gulp, and ran away.

Tom, however, was still not disheartened; and thinking the wolf would not dislike having some chat with him as he was going along, he called out, "My good friend, I can show you a famous treat." "Where's that?" said the wolf. "In such and such a house," said Tom, describing his own father's house. "You can crawl through the drain into the kitchen and then into the pantry, and there you will find cakes, ham, beef, cold chicken, roast pig, apple-dumplings, and everything that your heart can wish."

The wolf did not want to be asked twice; so that very night he went to the house and crawled through the drain into the kitchen, and then into the pantry, and ate and drank there to his heart's content. As soon as he had had enough he wanted to get away; but he had eaten so much that he could not go out by the same way he came in.

This was just what Tom had reckoned upon; and now he began to set up a great shout, making all the noise he could. "Will you be easy?" said the wolf; "you'll awaken everybody in the house if you make such a clatter." "What's that to me?" said the little man; "you have had your frolic, now I've a mind to be merry myself"; and he began singing and shouting as loud as he could.

The woodman and his wife, being awakened by the noise, peeped through a crack in the door; but when they saw a wolf was there, you may well suppose that they were sadly frightened; and the woodman ran for his axe, and gave his wife a scythe. "Do you stay behind," said the woodman, "and when I have knocked him on the head you must rip him up with the scythe." Tom heard all this, and cried out, "Father, father! I am here, the wolf has swallowed me." And his father said, "Heaven be praised! we have found our dear child again"; and he told his wife not to use the scythe for fear she should hurt him. Then he aimed a great blow, and struck the wolf on the head, and killed him on the spot! and when he was dead they cut open his body, and set Tommy free. "Ah!" said the father, "what fears we have had for you!" "Yes, father," answered he; "I have traveled all over the world, I think, in one way or other, since we parted; and now I am very glad to come home and get fresh air again." "Why, where have you been?" said his father. "I have been in a mouse-hole—and in a snail-shell—and down a cow's throat—and in the wolf's belly; and yet here I am again, safe and sound."

"Well," said they, "you are come back, and we will not sell you again for all the riches in the world."

Then they hugged and kissed their dear little son, and gave him plenty to eat and drink, for he was very hungry; and then they fetched new clothes for him, for his old ones had been quite spoiled on his journey. So Master Thumb stayed at home with his father and mother, in peace; for though he had been so great a traveler, and had done and seen so many fine things, and was fond enough of telling the whole story, he always agreed that, after all, there's no place like HOME!

"*A father carries pictures where his money used to be.*"

—AUTHOR UNKNOWN

SOCCER TERMS TO KNOW

When you watch sports games with your kids, they might want to know what certain terms mean so they can follow along. Here's a glossary of key soccer words.

CONTAINMENT The process of slowing down an attacker and keeping him in front of you as you back toward the goal.

CORNER KICK The free kick given to the attacking team when the defending team has kicked the ball over its own end line.

DEFENDER A player whose main job is to protect her own goal.

DRIBBLING A series of short, crisp taps on the ball that allows the soccer player to run with the ball under his control.

FIFA The Fédération Internationale de Football Association is the official soccer organization for world play. If a rule change is made, it's made by FIFA.

GIVE-AND-GO A way of getting around a defender by "bouncing" the ball off one of your teammates. Your teammate receives the ball while you run around the defender and then passes it back to you when you're free.

GOALKEEPER The only player on the field allowed to use his hands. This ability is restricted to the penalty-box area.

GOAL KICK The free kick awarded to the defending team when the attacking team has kicked the ball over the goal line.

HEADER When a player uses his head to direct the ball.

INDIRECT KICK The free kick given to a team when a player on the other team has committed a foul. This kick must be touched by two players before it can go into the goal.

JUGGLING Keeping the ball from touching the ground using your feet and thighs and even your head to pop the ball back up into the air.

MIDFIELDER A transition position between attack and defense.

OFFSIDES A violation of the rule that requires either the ball or two defenders be between an attacker and the goal.

PENALTY BOX The area in front of the goal inside the 18-yard line.

PENALTY KICK A free kick awarded when the defending team fouls inside the penalty box.

SHIELDING The process of keeping your body between the defender and the ball to prevent the defender from getting to the ball.

TRAPPING Stopping the soccer ball and getting it under control with any part of the body.

The House That Jack Built

This is the house that Jack built.
This is the malt
That lay in the house that Jack built.

This is the rat,
That ate the malt
That lay in the house that Jack built.

This is the cat,
That killed the rat,
That ate the malt
That lay in the house that Jack built.

This is the dog,
That worried the cat,
That killed the rat,
That ate the malt
That lay in the house that Jack built.

This is the cow with the crumpled horn,
That tossed the dog,
That worried the cat,
That killed the rat,
That ate the malt
That lay in the house that Jack built.

This is the maiden all forlorn,
That milked the cow with the crumpled horn,
That tossed the dog,
That worried the cat,
That killed the rat,
That ate the malt
That lay in the house that Jack built.

This is the man all tattered and torn,
That kissed the maiden all forlorn,
That milked the cow with the crumpled horn,
That tossed the dog,
That worried the cat,
That killed the rat,
That ate the malt
That lay in the house that Jack built.

This is the priest all shaven and shorn,
That married the man all tattered and torn,
That kissed the maiden all forlorn,
That milked the cow with the crumpled horn,
That tossed the dog,
That worried the cat,
That killed the rat,
That ate the malt
That lay in the house that Jack built.

This is the cock that crowed in the morn,
That waked the priest all shaven and shorn,
That married the man all tattered and torn,
That kissed the maiden all forlorn,
That milked the cow with the crumpled horn,
That tossed the dog,
That worried the cat,
That killed the rat,
That ate the malt
That lay in the house that Jack built.

This is the farmer sowing the corn,
That kept the cock that crowed in the morn.
That waked the priest all shaven and shorn,
That married the man all tattered and torn,
That kissed the maiden all forlorn,
That milked the cow with the crumpled horn,
That tossed the dog,
That worried the cat,
That killed the rat,
That ate the malt
That lay in the house that Jack built.

HOW TO PLAY KICK THE CAN

These games have been favorites of little boys for centuries. Share your fond memories with you son and teach him how to play these classics!

WHAT YOU'LL NEED:

At least four players

An empty tin can, soda can, or even an empty paint can or bucket (You can also use a ball, an empty plastic milk jug, or any other "kickable" object.)

A large, safe, open space, like a field or yard in which to play. (If supervised, it can also be played in a parking lot or at the end of a cul-de-sac.)

1. Draw straws or decide who the "counter" (also referred to as the jailor, ruler, seeker, or "it") will be. All other players will be "hiders."
2. The game begins with the "can" being set upright in the middle of the play area, and the counter closing his or her eyes and counting to a decided upon number. All of the other players hide.
3. The counter then sets out to find all the other players. If a player is found, the counter yells out that player's name and they race back to the can. If the hider kicks the can before the counter, the game starts again. But if the counter kicks the can first, then the hider is "caught," and he or she is sent "to the can" or "to jail", which is a designated area for the "captured" players, typically right near the can.

4. While the counter continues to look for players, the players can risk capture at any time and come out of hiding to try and kick the can. If a player can succeed without being tagged by the counter, the captives are set free from the can! The players then go hide again. But if the player is tagged before he or she can kick the can, he or she will be sent to the jail as well.

5. The game continues until the counter has captured all the players, or until a found hider beats the counter back to the can!

The Pied Piper of Hamelin

ONCE UPON A TIME on the banks of a great river in northern Germany was a town called Hamelin. The citizens of Hamelin were honest and content. Many peaceful, prosperous years passed until one day, an extraordinary thing happened to disturb the peace. Hamelin had always had many rats, but they had never been a danger, because the cats had always kept their numbers down. Suddenly, however, the rats began to multiply. In the end, a black sea of rats swarmed over the whole town. First, they attacked the barns and warehouses, then, they gnawed the wood, cloth, and everything else within their reach. The only thing they didn't eat was metal.

The terrified citizens begged the town councilors to free them from the plague of rats. But the council had, for a long time, been trying to think of a plan. "What we need is an army of cats!" But all of the cats were dead, they had all died from a strange illness the year before. "We'll put down poisoned food then . . . " But most of the food was already gone, and even poison did not stop the rats. The meeting was interrupted by a loud knock at the door.

"Who can that be?" the city fathers wondered. They opened the door and to their surprise there stood a tall thin man dressed in brightly colored clothes, with a long plume in his hat. He was waving a gold pipe at them.

"I've freed other towns of beetles, bats, and rats," the stranger proclaimed, "and for a thousand florins, I'll get rid of your rats!"

"A thousand florins!" exclaimed the mayor. "We'll give you one hundred thousand if you succeed!"

At once the stranger hurried away, saying, "It's late now, but at dawn tomorrow, there won't be a rat left in Hamelin!" The sun was still below the horizon, when the melodic sound of a pipe wafted through the streets of Hamelin. The pied piper slowly made his way through the houses, and behind him flocked the rats. Out they scampered from doors, windows, and gutters, rats of every size, all after the piper. As he played, he marched down to the river and straight into the water, up to his waist. Behind him swarmed the rats, and every one was drowned and swept away by the current. By the time the sun was high in the sky, there was not a single rat in the town. There was even greater delight at the town hall, until the piper tried to claim his payment.

"One hundred thousand florins?" exclaimed the councilors, "Never . . ."

"A thousand florins at least!" cried the pied piper angrily.

But the mayor broke in. "The rats are all dead now and they can never come back. So be grateful for fifty florins, or you'll not get even that."

His eyes flashing with rage, the pied piper waved a threatening finger at the mayor. "You'll bitterly regret ever breaking your promise," he said, and vanished.

A shiver of fear ran through the councilors, but the mayor shrugged and said excitedly, "We've saved nine hundred and fifty florins!"

That night, freed from the nightmare of the rats, the citizens of Hamelin slept more soundly than ever. And when the strange sound of piping wafted through the streets at dawn, only the children heard it. Drawn as if by magic, they hurried out of their homes. Again, the pied piper paced through the town, this time, it was children of all shapes and sizes who flocked at his heels to the sound of his strange piping. The long procession soon left the town and made its way through the wood and across the forest, until it reached the foot of a huge mountain. When the piper came to the dark rock, he played his pipe even louder still, and a giant door opened. Beyond it was a cave. In went the children behind the pied piper, and when the last child had gone into the darkness, the door slowly shut.

A great landslide came down the mountain blocking the entrance to the cave forever. Only one little lame boy escaped this fate, and he told the anxious citizens of Hamelin who were searching for their children what had happened.

No matter what the people did, the mountain never gave up its victims. Many years were to pass before the merry voices of other children would ring through the streets of Hamelin, but the memory of the harsh lesson remained etched in everyone's heart and was passed down through the generations.

CLASSIC CARD GAME: I DOUBT IT

*If you're good at bluffing, I Doubt It is the game for you
and your family! It helps to develop counting skills and
the ability to recognize the value of cards.*

This game requires two or more players, using
a standard deck of fifty-two cards.

OBJECTIVE:

To be the first to get rid of your stack of cards.

1. A random dealer is selected who deals out the entire deck evenly to the players. Play begins with the youngest player laying any number of aces in her hand face down on the table. As she lays them down, she calls out what they are ("Two aces"). The next player then discards any or all of his twos, the next player his threes, and so on until kings are played. After you play kings, play continues on again to aces.

2. Since you are laying your cards face down, you can actually bluff your opponents. You can lay down a four but say that you are laying down a ten. If you believe that another player did not lay down the cards he said he did, yell out "I doubt it!" The player then has to turn over the cards he laid down. If they are indeed the cards he said they were, you must pick up the entire pile of discarded cards. If the cards are different than what he said, he must pick up the pile of discarded cards himself!

3. The first player to get rid of her cards wins the game. Since the game ends when the first player gets rid of his hand, a player will undoubtedly yell "I doubt it" when you lay your last card. Make sure that it's a correct call, or you'll be stuck picking up the discards and possibly losing!

"The heart of a father is the master-piece of nature."

—ANTOINE-FRANÇOIS, ABBÉ PRÉVOST D'EXILES

JUST FOR LAUGHS

Knock knock!
Who's there?
Pudding.
Pudding who?
Pudding your shoes on before
   your pants is a silly idea!

Knock knock!
Who's there?
Stan.
Stan who?
Stan back, I'm coming
   through!

Knock knock!
Who's there?
Cockadoodle.
Cockadoodle who?
Cockadoodle doo, not cocka-
   doodle who!

Knock knock!
Who's there?
One shoe.
One shoe who?
One shoe come over for a
   while?

Knock knock!
Who's there?
Wanda.
Wanda who?
Wanda bough breaks, the
   baby will fall!

Knock knock!
Who's there?
Wooden.
Wooden who?
Wooden you like to find out!

Knock knock!
Who's there?
Major.
Major who?
Major look!

Knock knock!
Who's there?
Howard.
Howard who?
Howard I know?

Knock knock!
Who's there?
Hyde.
Hyde who?
Hyde like to tell you another
   joke!

Knock knock!
Who's there?
Alaska.
Alaska who?
Alaska once more and that's
   it!

Knock knock!
Who's there?
Diploma.
Diploma who?
Diploma is coming to fix the
   pipes!

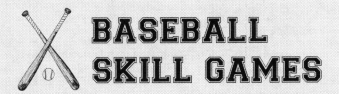

BASEBALL SKILL GAMES

HITTING

- This one's simple: Take a bucket of balls out to an empty field. Pitch some balls to your children and have them practice hitting.
- Get some Wiffle balls. (Wiffle balls are plastic balls with holes in them.) Since they won't go far, they are less likely to hurt someone or something. Wiffle balls are good for playing on a small field or in the backyard.
- Hit balls off of a tee. Your children can practice hitting the ball in different directions: Try having them hit ten balls to left field, ten to center field, then ten to right field.
- Go to a batting cage. A machine will pitch a ball to your child, and you can decide how fast you want the ball to come. Since you won't be pitching, you can better help your child with his stance and swing.

THROWING

- Grab your gloves and play catch. Don't throw as hard or as fast as you can; just stand at a comfortable distance and practice throwing the ball right to your child. See how many throws you can make to each other without dropping the ball. Once you can make 30 or 40 throws in a row, each of you take a big step back and try again.

FIELDING GROUND BALLS

- Hit some ground balls to your child. Start by making sure he or she can catch the ball every time. Tell your child to shuffle her feet to get her body in front of the ball; watch the ball all the way until it is inside the glove. Try to set her in such a good position that anytime the ball takes a funny hop it hits her in the leg or in the chest and stops nearby. That way she'll still be able to pick the ball up quickly.
- Set up some bases. Put one person at bat, one person at first base, and one person at shortstop. Have the batter hit ground balls toward the shortstop, who should field them and throw to first base. Keep this up until the shortstop successfully fields five or ten balls in a row, then rotate who gets to play shortstop.
- Practice grounders by throwing a tennis ball against a wall and having your child field the rebound.

CATCHING FLY BALLS

- Fly ball practice is best done with a real batter, not just with someone throwing the ball in the air. Hit fly balls to your children.

PITCHING

- The best youth league and even high school pitchers don't necessarily throw hard or curvy stuff. They throw a fastball consistently to the catcher's glove every time. So first and foremost, help your children focus on their aim.
- Try teaching him a changeup. You normally grip a fastball with your thumb and your first two fingers. Instead, have him try holding the ball all the way back in his palm, but using the same

arm motion as he does for a fastball. He should find that this pitch goes just a bit slower; that's a changeup. Changeups are hard to hit because they throw off the batter's timing—the batter will be starting to swing just before the ball gets to the plate.

HOW TO TIE CLASSIC KNOTS

Whether you and your children are securing a dingy, tying a fishing lure, or hauling something in the back of your pickup truck, it's fun to show them some common knot styles.

OVERHAND KNOT

This knot has several names. You may hear it called Simple Overhand Knot. If you use thread or other small cordage to tie this knot, it is called the Thumb Knot. When tied with two cords, as when you start tying shoelaces, it is called the Half Knot.

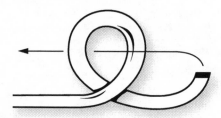

1. Pass the running end around the standing part, making a loop, and then pass it through the crossing turn.

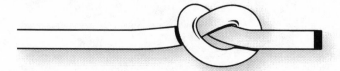

2. Tighten the knot by pulling on both the standing part and the running end.

Besides being the foundation of many different knots, the Overhand Knot has many distinct properties of its own. For example, it weakens most cordage it is tied in by 50 percent or more, and tightening it down can damage the fibers of some ropes. Consequently, it is tied in nylon fishing line to test for brittleness. If fishing line has lost any of its flexibility, it will break very easily as you tie an Overhand Knot in it and tighten it with a quick jerk from both sides. Fishermen take care not to accidentally let an Overhand Knot form in their line so as not to lose half its strength. Once it's tied, the knot is difficult to undo. It should only be tied in small cordage or thread if it is not meant to be untied.

SLIPPED NOOSE

This knot is similar to the Overhand Knot. The difference is that the last tuck is made with a bight of the standing part, instead of the running end.

Pass the running end around the standing part, making a loop; then, make a bight in the standing part and pass it through the crossing turn. Pull on the running end and on the bight loop to tighten.

It is important to learn the difference between the Overhand Knot and the Slipped Noose. Each one will serve you as the starting point for other knots.

FIGURE EIGHT KNOT

This knot is started like the Overhand Knot, but here the running end makes a complete round turn around the standing part before passing through its loop.

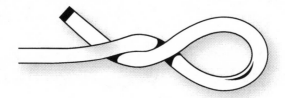

1. Use the running end to make a crossing turn, and pass the end under the standing part.

2. Twist the running end up and through the crossing turn.

3. Tighten the knot by pulling on both ends.

If you wish to use the Figure Eight Knot as a stopper knot, modify Step 2 by pulling the standing part while pressing against the base of the knot on that side. When the Figure Eight Knot and similar stopper knots are tightened this way, the running end will point to the side at a right angle.

The Figure Eight Knot is frequently used as a basis for other knots. It is much easier to untie than the Overhand Knot, and is not as damaging to rope fibers. Because the Figure Eight Knot has a distinctive "figure eight" look, it's easy to check to make sure it's tied correctly. This is one of the reasons it is popular with rescue work. It is used on the running rigging of sailboats to keep lines from running all the way through leads and pulleys.

FISHERMAN'S KNOT

Even though this is really a bend, it is known as the Fisherman's Knot, Englishman's Knot, and the Angler's Knot.

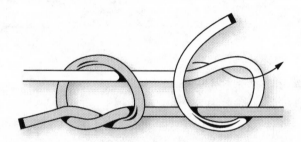

1. Lay two ropes parallel to each other and overlap each rope's running end around the other's standing part, making two Overhand Knots.

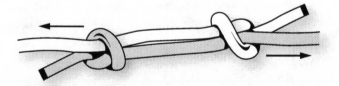

2. Tighten each Overhand by pulling on the two standing parts, so that the two ropes are held firmly together.

3. Pull the two ropes apart so that they form a circle, tightening each knot.

The Fisherman's Knot is difficult to untie and will work best when tied in small cordage. It is often chosen as a secure way to join two small lines of similar size.

HALF HITCH

There are two basic ways of making a Half Hitch. It can be tied off with a running end, or it can be tied off with a bight, which makes it a Slipped Half Hitch.

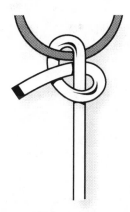

1. Bring the running end around the ring or post and then around its standing part. Then, tuck the end inside the crossing turn, next to the ring.

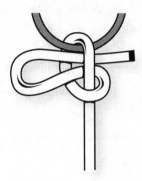

2. Another option is to make the last tuck with a bight, making it a Slipped Half Hitch.

The Half Hitch makes a very quick and temporary tie off. It is also tied as the first step of other more secure hitches. The slipped version unties completely with just one pull.

IMPROVED CLINCH KNOT

This knot is a useful fishing knot that works well with thin monofilament.

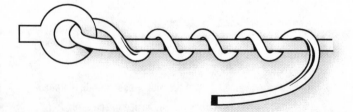

1. Pass the running end through the hook eye or other attachment point, then make three to five wraps around the standing part.

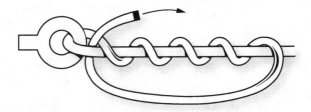

2. Bring the running end back and thread it through the crossing turn closest to the eye.

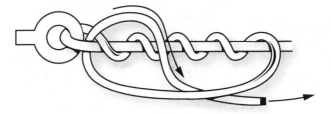

3. Tuck the running end through its own bight. Tighten the knot by pulling on the standing part. If there's slack, take it out by pulling on the running end.

If the last tuck is not made, what you have is the simple Clinch Knot. Thin monofilament requires more wraps than thicker line does, and even one wrap can make the difference in whether it slips under strain. It is difficult to pull this knot down when tied in thick line.

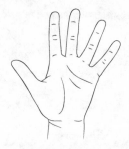

One, Two, Three

One, two, three, four, five,
Once I caught a fish alive.
Six, seven, eight, nine, ten,
But I let it go again.
Why did you let it go?
Because it bit my finger so.
Which finger did it bite?
The little one upon the right.

Three Wise Men of Gotham

Three wise men of Gotham
Went to sea in a bowl;
If the bowl had been stronger
My song would be longer.

The Three Billy Goats Gruff

Reader tip: "The Three Billy Goats Gruff" is an excellent fairy tale to read aloud to your children because there are so many interesting voices. Make your voice tiny and meek when reading the words of the smallest goat. Make your voice loud and fierce when reading the words of the biggest Billy Goat Gruff.

ONCE UPON A TIME there were three billy goats that lived in a village in Scandinavia. One day, their owner sent them down the road and up to the hillside to graze and fatten up. For you see, these three billy goats had rather a nice life. They lived on a farm where they had occasional chores to do. Other than these little odd jobs, they were free to play games and graze, their favorite occupation of all. All of these billy goats were named "Gruff."

So, following their owner's orders, they set off down the road toward the hill where they were to graze. They were eager to get there because this rolling hill had particularly sweet grass growing on it.

On the way up the hill there was a small bridge they had to cross. Now, under the bridge, as everyone in the village knew, lived a great ugly troll, with eyes as big as saucers and a nose as long as a baseball bat. He was an awful looking creature!

When the three goats arrived at the bridge, they decided that the youngest should cross first.

So, off went the youngest Billy Goat Gruff to cross the bridge.

"Trip, trap! Trip, trap!" went the goat, lightly tripping over the bridge.

"Who's that tripping over my bridge?" roared the troll, who had been napping and was very cross at having been disturbed.

"Oh, it's only me," said the tiniest Billy Goat Gruff, who was a bit afraid of that roaring creature, "and I'm going up to the hill to graze on some grass."

"Oh, no you're not, because I'm coming out to gobble you up," said the ill-behaved troll.

"Oh, no! Please don't take me. I'm too little," said the billy goat in a wee, quivering voice. "Wait a bit until the second Billy Goat Gruff comes, he's much bigger, probably tastier, too."

"Well, be off with you, then," said the troll, who, come to think of it, was feeling quite hungry and thought that bigger probably would be better in choosing a goat meal.

Soon came the second Billy Goat Gruff, setting out to cross the bridge.

"Trip, trap! Trip, trap! Trip, trap!" went the goat on the bridge, not nearly as light on his feet as the first Billy Goat Gruff.

"Who is that tripping over my bridge?" roared the troll.

"Oh, it's only the second Billy Goat Gruff, and I'm going up to the hill to eat some grass. The grass on that hill is particularly tasty," said the billy goat, a bit troubled by the gruesome voice from under the bridge.

"Oh, no you don't—I'm coming out from under the bridge to gobble you up," said the troll, who by now really was getting quite hungry and crabby.

"Please, don't take me, wait a little while until the oldest Billy Goat Gruff comes, he's much bigger. He'll be the best meal of all. Tasty and substantial," said the second Billy Goat Gruff.

"Okay! Get away then," said the troll, already drooling at the thought of a really large and delicious goat meal. Just as he was thinking about this prospect up came the biggest Billy Goat Gruff.

"TRIP, TRAP! TRIP, TRAP! TRIP, TRAP!" went the bridge, for the billy goat was so heavy that the bridge, which wasn't very sturdy anyway, practically buckled under him.

"WHO'S THAT TRAMPING OVER MY BRIDGE?" roared the troll, very hungry and very crabby by now.

"It is the big Billy Goat Gruff and I am going to graze on the hill across the bridge," roared the billy goat, who had an ugly, hoarse voice of his own, one to match that of the troll.

"You think so, do you? Well, think again. I'm coming out from under by bridge to gobble you all up," roared the troll.

"Well, come along then! I've got two spears and I'll use them to poke your eyeballs out. And, I've got two curling-stones, and I'll crush you to bits," answered the third Billy Goat Gruff who was not at all scared of this little troll creature.

Well, true to his word, the troll ran out from under the bridge, ready to eat the biggest Billy Goat Gruff. But this big goat flew at the troll, and poked his eyes out with his horns. Then he crushed him to bits, body and bones, and tossed him back under the bridge. After that, he calmly went up the hillside where he joined the other two Billy Goats Gruff and told them what had happened. On that hillside, the Billy Goats Gruff got so fat they were hardly able to walk home again.

HOW TO PLAY FOUR SQUARE

This classic playground game is easy to replicate at home.

WHAT YOU'LL NEED:

At least four people

Chalk or tape

A rubber playground ball

A flat concrete surface like a patio or driveway on which to play

1. Make or draw a large ten-foot-square "court" and divide it into four equal quadrants. Number these smaller squares 1, 2, 3, and 4. Square 1 is the highest-ranking square; square 4 is the lowest. Make a diagonal line across the outside corner of square 1 to create a small triangle; this is where the ball will be served from. The goal is to move up by eliminating other players; to stay in, or move into, the number 1 square.

2. The player in square 1 begins by serving the ball into any other square. The ball must bounce once and the player in that square must hit the ball with his or her hand(s) into another square. The game continues until a player

   - Misses a ball
   - Hits a ball out of bounds
   - Allows the ball to bounce more than once in the square
   - Hits the ball into the player's own square
   - Catches or holds the ball instead of hitting it

A player who makes any of these errors is eliminated, and players move up accordingly into the next highest-ranking square. If there are more than four players, the new players step into the lowest square as players are eliminated.

2. The winner is the last person left, or whoever holds the server's position the longest in square 1!

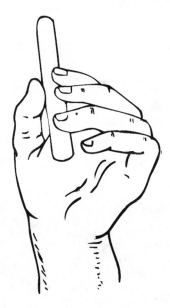

"*When a father gives to his son, both laugh; when a son gives to his father, both cry.*"

—WILLIAM SHAKESPEARE

BASKETBALL TERMS TO KNOW

When you watch sports games with your kids, they might want to know what certain terms mean so they can follow along. Here's a glossary of key basketball words.

CENTER The tallest player on the team, counted on to score baskets from in close, to win jump balls, block opposing players' shots, and get a lot of rebounds.

CHARGE When an offensive player runs into a defender whose feet are planted.

DEFENSIVE REBOUND If your opponent misses a shot and you get the ball, it is a defensive rebound because it came at the end of the court you are defending.

DRIBBLING Bouncing the ball up and down—required to move with the basketball.

FADEAWAY JUMPER Jumping backward at a slight angle while taking a shot. It is very hard to block.

FAST BREAK Moving the ball quickly up the court and not allowing defensive players to set up. Often results in outnumbering the defensive team momentarily if done fast, allowing a player an open or unguarded attempt to score.

FIELD GOAL Any shot other than a free throw.

FIVE-SECOND VIOLATION When inbounding the ball, the player trying to do it has to pass the ball inbounds within five seconds or the opposing team gets possession.

FOUL LINE The line 15 feet in front of the basket where free throws are attempted.

FOUL OUT Depending on the level of play, five or six fouls result in the player no longer being allowed to play in that particular game.

FREE THROW Shots taken after a foul by the opposing team. The game is stopped and the player is allowed to shoot one, two, or as many as three uncontested free throws, which are always worth one point each.

JUMP BALL The ball is tossed in the air and the best jumpers or tallest players from each team jump and try to tip it to a teammate; used to start a game.

JUMP SHOT Used with a field goal; the player jumps, usually straight up, as part of the shooting motion so that a defender cannot block the shot. This replaced the set shot.

KEY The shaded rectangular area in front of each basket that goes out to the foul line, shooting line, and half-circle where players stand to shoot free throws.

LAYUP A two-point shot made from in close from either side of the basket, banked off the glass and into the basket. One of the most successful shots attempted if the player is open; however, it is also often blocked by taller players. Though often done off a fastbreak, it can also be done when a player becomes open near the basket.

PICK AND ROLL A player sets a screen (also called a pick) for the ball handler, then the screen setter slips behind the defender to get a pass from the ball handler.

POINT GUARD The Number 1 spot on the floor, the player who dribbles the ball up the court and sets up the offense. Though there are now taller point guards, traditionally the point guard is smaller, has good knowledge of the game, and gets a lot of assists by finding the open teammate to set up baskets.

POST UP Taking a position close to the basket, facing away from the basket, and getting between the defender and the teammate with the ball to create a passing lane to receive the ball.

POWER FORWARD Referred to as the Number 4 spot. A power forward can rebound and play inside and has the size and strength to get a lot of offensive and defensive rebounds, but score a lot on offense.

REBOUND Getting the ball after it hits the rim on an unsuccessful shot on either the defensive or offensive end.

SHOT CLOCK Used to speed up the pace of a game and prevent teams with a lead from stalling or running out the clock. Forces teams to take a shot that at least hits the rim (or goes in) within a set amount of time, usually 24 seconds or 30 seconds, but occasionally 35 depending on the level of play. If a team fails to take a shot that at least hits the rim in the allotted time, the other team gets the ball.

TRIPLE-DOUBLE Getting 10 or more points each in scoring, rebounds, and assists.

Aladdin and the Wonderful Lamp

THERE ONCE LIVED a poor tailor, who had a son called Aladdin, a careless, idle boy who would do nothing but play ball all day long in the streets with little idle boys like himself. This so grieved the father that he died; yet, in spite of his mother's tears and prayers, Aladdin did not mend his ways. One day, when he was playing in the streets as usual, a stranger asked him his age, and if he was not the son of Mustapha the tailor. "I am, sir," replied Aladdin; "but he died a long while ago." On this the stranger, who was a famous African magician, fell on his neck and kissed him, saying, "I am your uncle, and knew you from your likeness to my brother. Go to your mother and tell her I am coming." Aladdin ran home and told his mother of his newly found uncle. "Indeed, child," she said, "your father had a brother, but I always thought he was dead." However, she prepared supper, and bade Aladdin seek his uncle, who came laden with wine and fruit. He presently fell down and kissed the place where Mustapha used to sit, bidding Aladdin's mother not to be surprised at not having seen him before, as he had been forty years out of the country. He then turned to Aladdin, and asked him his trade, at which the boy hung his head, while his mother burst into tears. On learning that Aladdin was idle and would learn no trade, he offered to take a shop for him and stock it with merchandise. Next day he bought Aladdin a fine suit of clothes and took him all over the city, showing him the sights, and brought him home at nightfall to his mother, who was overjoyed to see her son so fine.

The next day the magician led Aladdin into some beautiful gardens a long way outside the city gates. They sat down by a fountain and the magician pulled a cake from his girdle, which he divided between them. They then journeyed onward till they almost reached the mountains. Aladdin was so tired that he begged to go back, but the magician beguiled him with pleasant stories, and led him on in spite of himself. At last they came to two mountains divided by a narrow valley. "We will go no farther," said the false uncle. "I will show you something wonderful; only do you gather up sticks while I kindle a fire." When it was lit the magician threw on it a powder he had about him, at the same time saying some magical words. The earth trembled a little and opened in front of them, disclosing a square flat stone with a brass ring in the middle to raise it by. Aladdin tried to run away, but the magician caught him and gave him a blow that knocked him down. "What have I done, uncle?" he said piteously; whereupon the magician said more kindly: "Fear nothing, but obey me. Beneath this stone lies a treasure which is to be yours, and no one else may touch it, so you must do exactly as I tell you." At the word treasure Aladdin forgot his fears, and grasped the ring as he was told, saying the names of his father and grandfather. The stone came up quite easily, and some steps appeared. "Go down," said the magician; "at the foot of those steps you will find an open door leading into three large halls. Tuck up your gown and go through them without touching anything, or you will die instantly. These halls lead into a garden of fine fruit trees. Walk on until you come to a niche in a terrace where stands a lighted lamp. Pour out the oil it contains, and bring it to me." He drew a ring from his finger and gave it to Aladdin, bidding him prosper.

Aladdin found everything as the magician had said, gathered some fruit off the trees, and, having got the lamp, arrived at the mouth of the cave. The magician cried out in a great hurry: "Make haste and give me the lamp." This Aladdin refused to do until he was out of the cave. The magician flew into a terrible passion, and throwing some more powder on to the fire, he said something, and the stone rolled back into its place.

The magician left Persia for ever, which plainly showed that he was no uncle of Aladdin's, but a cunning magician, who had read in his magic books of a wonderful lamp, which would make him the most powerful man in the world. Though he alone knew where to find it, he could only receive it from the hand of another. He had picked out the foolish Aladdin for this purpose, intending to get the lamp and kill him afterward.

For two days Aladdin remained in the dark, crying and lamenting. At last he clasped his hands in prayer, and in so doing rubbed the ring, which the magician had forgotten to take from him. Immediately an enormous and frightful genie rose out of the earth, saying: "What wouldst thou with me? I am the Slave of the Ring, and will obey thee in all things." Aladdin fearlessly replied: "Deliver me from this place!" whereupon the earth opened, and he found himself outside. As soon as his eyes could bear the light he went home, but fainted on the threshold. When he came to himself he told his mother what had passed, and showed her the lamp and the fruits he had gathered in the garden, which were, in reality, precious stones. He then asked for some food. "Alas! child," she said, "I have nothing in the house, but I have spun a little cotton and will go and sell it." Aladdin bade her keep her cotton, for he would sell the lamp instead. As it was very dirty she began to rub it, that it might fetch a higher price. Instantly a hideous genie appeared, and asked what she would have. She fainted away, but Aladdin, snatching the lamp, said boldly: "Fetch me something to eat!" The genie returned with a silver bowl, twelve silver plates containing rich meats, two silver cups, and two bottles of wine. Aladdin's mother, when she came to herself, said: "Whence comes this splendid feast?" "Ask not, but eat," replied Aladdin. So they sat at breakfast till it was dinnertime, and Aladdin told his mother about the lamp. She begged him to sell it, and have nothing to do with devils. "No," said Aladdin, "since chance hath made us aware of its virtues, we will use it, and the ring likewise, which I shall always wear on my finger." When they had eaten all the genie had brought, Aladdin sold one of the silver plates, and so on until none were left. He then had recourse to the genie, who gave him another set of plates, and thus they lived for many years.

One day Aladdin heard an order from the Sultan proclaimed that everyone was to stay at home and close his shutters while the Princess, his daughter, went to and from the bath. Aladdin was seized by a desire to see her face, which was very difficult, as she always went veiled. He hid himself behind the door of the bath, and peeped through a chink. The Princess lifted her veil as she went in, and looked so beautiful that Aladdin fell in love with her at first sight. He went home so changed that his mother was frightened. He told her he loved the Princess so deeply that he could not live without her, and meant to ask her in marriage of her father. His mother, on hearing this, burst out laughing, but Aladdin at last prevailed upon her to go before the Sultan and carry his request. She fetched a napkin and laid in it the magic fruits from the enchanted garden, which sparkled and shone like the most beautiful jewels. She took these with her to please the Sultan, and set out, trusting in the lamp. The Grand Vizier and the lords of council had just gone in as she entered the hall and placed herself in front of the Sultan. He, however, took no notice of her. She went every day for a week, and stood in the same place. When the council broke up on the sixth day the Sultan said to his Vizier: "I see a certain woman in the audience-chamber every day carrying something in a napkin. Call her next time, that I may find out what she wants." Next day, at a sign from the Vizier, she went up to the foot of the throne and remained kneeling till the Sultan said to her: "Rise, good woman, and tell me what you want." She hesitated, so the Sultan sent away all but the Vizier, and bade her speak frankly, promising to forgive her beforehand for anything she might say. She then told him of her son's violent love for the Princess. "I prayed him to forget her," she said, "but in vain; he threatened to do some desperate deed if I refused to go and ask your Majesty for the hand of the Princess. Now I pray you to forgive not me alone, but my son Aladdin." The Sultan asked her kindly what she had in the napkin, whereupon she unfolded the jewels and presented them. He was thunderstruck, and turning to the Vizier said: "What sayest thou? Ought I not to bestow the Princess on one who values her at such a price?" The Vizier, who wanted her for his own son, begged the Sultan to withhold her for three months, in the course of which he hoped his son would contrive to make him a richer present. The Sultan granted this, and told Aladdin's mother that, though he consented to the marriage, she must not appear before him again for three months.

Aladdin waited patiently for nearly three months, but after two had elapsed his mother, going into the city to buy oil, found every one rejoicing, and asked what was going on. "Do you not know," was the answer, "that the son of the Grand Vizier is to marry the Sultan's daughter to-night?" Breathless, she ran and told Aladdin, who was overwhelmed at first, but presently bethought him of the lamp. He rubbed it, and the genie appeared, saying, "What is thy will?" Aladdin replied: "The Sultan, as thou knowest, has broken his promise to me, and the Vizier's son is to have the Princess. My command is that to-night you bring hither the bride and bridegroom." "Master, I obey," said the genie. Aladdin then went to his chamber, where, sure enough, at midnight the genie transported the bed containing the Vizier's son and the Princess. "Take this new-married man," he said, "and put him outside in the cold, and return at daybreak." Whereupon the genie took the Vizier's son out of bed, leaving Aladdin with the Princess. "Fear nothing," Aladdin said to her; "you are my wife, promised to me by your unjust father, and no harm shall come to you." The Princess was too frightened to speak, and passed the most miserable night of her life, while Aladdin lay down beside her and slept soundly. At the appointed hour the genie fetched in the shivering bridegroom, laid him in his place, and transported the bed back to the palace.

Presently the Sultan came to wish his daughter good morning. The unhappy Vizier's son jumped up and hid himself, while the Princess would not say a word, and was very sorrowful. The Sultan sent her mother to her, who said: "How comes it, child, that you will not speak to your father? What has happened?" The Princess sighed deeply, and at last told her mother how, during the night, the bed had been carried into some strange house, and what had passed there. Her mother did not believe her in the least, but bade her rise and consider it an idle dream.

The following night exactly the same thing happened, and next morning, on the Princess's refusal to speak, the Sultan threatened to cut off her head. She then confessed all, bidding him to ask the Vizier's son if it were not so. The Sultan told the Vizier to ask his son, who owned the truth, adding that, dearly as he loved the Princess, he had rather die than go through another such fearful night, and wished to be separated from her. His wish was granted, and there was an end to feasting and rejoicing.

When the three months were over, Aladdin sent his mother to remind the Sultan of his promise. She stood in the same place as before, and the Sultan, who had forgotten Aladdin, at once remembered him, and sent for her. On seeing her poverty the Sultan felt less inclined than ever to keep his word, and asked his Vizier's advice, who counseled him to set so high a value on the Princess that no man living could come up to it. The Sultan then turned to Aladdin's mother, saying: "Good woman, a Sultan must remember his promises, and I will remember mine, but your son must first send me forty basins of gold brimful of jewels, carried by forty black slaves, led by as many white ones, splendidly dressed. Tell him that I await his answer." The mother of Aladdin bowed low and went home, thinking all was lost. She gave Aladdin the message, adding: "He may wait long enough for your answer!" "Not so long, mother, as you think," her son replied. "I would do a great deal more than that for the Princess." He summoned the genie, and in a few moments the eighty slaves arrived, and filled up the small house and garden. Aladdin made them set out to the palace, two and two, followed by his mother. They were so richly dressed, with such splendid jewels in their girdles, that everyone crowded to see them and the basins of gold they carried on their heads. They entered the palace, and, after kneeling before the Sultan, stood in a half-circle round the throne with their arms crossed, while Aladdin's mother presented them to the Sultan. He hesitated no longer, but said: "Good woman, return and tell your son that I wait for him with open arms." She lost no time in telling Aladdin, bidding him make haste. But Aladdin first called the genie. "I want a scented bath," he said, "a richly embroidered habit, a horse surpassing the Sultan's, and twenty slaves to attend me. Besides this, six slaves, beautifully dressed, to wait on my mother; and lastly, ten thousand pieces of gold in ten purses." No sooner said than done. Aladdin mounted his horse and passed through the streets, the slaves strewing gold as they went. Those who had played with him in his childhood knew him not, he had grown so handsome. When the Sultan saw him he came down from his throne, embraced him, and led him into a hall where a feast was spread, intending to marry him to the Princess that very day. But Aladdin refused, saying, "I must build a palace fit for her," and took his leave. Once home, he said to the genie: "Build me a palace of the finest marble, set with jasper, agate, and other precious stones. In the middle you shall build me a large hall with a dome, its four walls of massy gold and silver, each having six windows, whose lattices, all except one which is to be left unfinished, must be set with diamonds and rubies. There must be stables and horses and grooms and slaves; go and see about it!"

The palace was finished by the next day, and the genie carried him there and showed him all his orders faithfully carried out, even to the laying of a velvet carpet from Aladdin's palace to the Sultan's. Aladdin's mother then dressed herself carefully, and walked to the palace with her slaves, while he followed her on horseback. The Sultan sent musicians with trumpets and cymbals to meet them, so that the air resounded with music and cheers. She was taken to the Princess, who saluted her and treated her with great honor. At night the Princess said goodbye to her father, and set out on the carpet for Aladdin's palace, with his mother at her side, and followed by the hundred slaves. She was charmed at the sight of Aladdin, who ran to receive her. "Princess," he said, "blame your beauty for my boldness if I have displeased you." She told him that, having seen him, she willingly obeyed her father in this matter. After the wedding had taken place Aladdin led her into the hall, where a feast was spread, and she supped with him, after which they danced till midnight. Next day Aladdin invited the Sultan to see the palace. On entering the hall with the four-and-twenty windows, with their rubies, diamonds, and emeralds, he cried: "It is a world's wonder! There is only one thing that surprises me. Was it by accident that one window was left unfinished?" "No, sir, by design," returned Aladdin. "I wished your Majesty to have the glory of finishing this palace." The Sultan was pleased, and sent for the best jewelers in the city. He showed them the unfinished window, and bade them fit it up like the others. "Sir," replied their spokesman, "we cannot find jewels enough." The Sultan had his own fetched, which they soon used, but to no purpose, for in a month's time the work was not half done. Aladdin, knowing that their task was vain, bade them undo their work and carry the jewels back, and the genie finished the window at his command. The Sultan was surprised to receive his jewels again, and visited Aladdin, who showed him the window finished. The Sultan embraced him, the envious Vizier meanwhile hinting that it was the work of enchantment.

Aladdin had won the hearts of the people by his gentle bearing. He was made captain of the Sultan's armies, and won several battles for him, but remained modest and courteous as before, and lived thus in peace and content for several years.

But far away in Africa the magician remembered Aladdin, and by his magic arts discovered that Aladdin, instead of perishing miserably in the cave, had escaped, and had married a princess, with whom he was living in great honor and wealth. He knew that the poor tailor's son could only have accomplished this by means of the lamp, and traveled night and day until he reached the capital of China, bent on Aladdin's ruin. As he passed through the town he heard people talking everywhere about a marvelous palace. "Forgive my ignorance," he asked, "what is this palace you speak of?" "Have you not heard of Prince Aladdin's palace," was the reply, "the greatest wonder of the world? I will direct you if you have a mind to see it." The magician thanked him who spoke, and having seen the palace, knew that it had been raised by the Genie of the Lamp, and became half mad with rage. He determined to get hold of the lamp, and again plunge Aladdin into the deepest poverty.

Unluckily, Aladdin had gone a-hunting for eight days, which gave the magician plenty of time. He bought a dozen copper lamps, put them into a basket, and went to the palace, crying: "New lamps for old!" followed by a jeering crowd. The Princess, sitting in the hall of four-and-twenty windows, sent a slave to find out what the noise was about, who came back laughing, so that the Princess scolded her. "Madam," replied the slave, "who can help laughing to see an old fool offering to exchange fine new lamps for old ones?" Another slave, hearing this, said: "There is an old one on the cornice there which he can have." Now this was the magic lamp, which Aladdin had left there, as he could not take it out hunting with him. The Princess, not knowing its value, laughingly bade the slave take it and make the exchange. She went and said to the magician: "Give me a new lamp for this." He snatched it and bade the slave take her choice, amid the jeers of the crowd. Little he cared, but left off crying his lamps, and went out of the city gates to a lonely place, where he remained till nightfall, when he pulled out the lamp and rubbed it. The genie appeared, and at the magician's command carried him, together with the palace and the Princess in it, to a lonely place in Africa.

Next morning the Sultan looked out of the window toward Aladdin's palace and rubbed his eyes, for it was gone. He sent for the Vizier and asked what had become of the palace. The Vizier looked out too, and was lost in astonishment. He again put it down to enchantment, and this time the Sultan believed him, and sent thirty men on horseback to fetch Aladdin in chains. They met him riding home, bound him, and forced him to go with them on foot. The people, however, who loved him, followed, armed, to see that he came to no harm. He was carried before the Sultan, who ordered the executioner to cut off his head. The executioner made Aladdin kneel down, bandaged his eyes, and raised his scimitar to strike. At that instant the Vizier, who saw that the crowd had forced their way into the courtyard and were scaling the walls to rescue Aladdin, called to the executioner to stay his hand. The people, indeed, looked so threatening that the Sultan gave way and ordered Aladdin to be unbound, and pardoned him in the sight of the crowd. Aladdin now begged to know what he had done. "False wretch!" said the Sultan, "come thither," and showed him from the window the place where his palace had stood. Aladdin was so amazed that he could not say a word. "Where is my palace and my daughter?" demanded the Sultan. "For the first I am not so deeply concerned, but my daughter I must have, and you must find her or lose your head." Aladdin begged for forty days in which to find her, promising, if he failed, to return and suffer death at the Sultan's pleasure. His prayer was granted, and he went forth sadly from the Sultan's presence. For three days he wandered about like a madman, asking everyone what had become of his palace, but they only laughed and pitied him. He came to the banks of a river, and knelt down to say his prayers before throwing himself in. In so doing he rubbed the magic ring he still wore. The genie he had seen in the cave appeared, and asked his will. "Save my life, genie," said Aladdin, "bring my palace back." "That is not in my power," said the genie; "I am only the Slave of the Ring; you must ask him of the lamp." "Even so," said Aladdin, "but thou canst take me to the palace, and set me down under my dear wife's window." He at once found himself in Africa, under the window of the Princess, and fell asleep out of sheer weariness.

He was awakened by the singing of the birds, and his heart was lighter. He saw plainly that all his misfortunes were owing to the loss of the lamp, and vainly wondered who had robbed him of it.

That morning the Princess rose earlier than she had done since she had been carried into Africa by the magician, whose company she was forced to endure once a day. She, however, treated him so harshly that he dared not live there altogether. As she was dressing, one of her women looked out and saw Aladdin. The Princess ran and opened the window, and at the noise she made Aladdin looked up. She called to him to come to her, and great was the joy of these lovers at seeing each other again. After he had kissed her Aladdin said: "I beg of you, Princess, in God's name, before we speak of anything else, for your own sake and mine, tell me what has become of an old lamp I left on the cornice in the hall of four-and-twenty windows, when I went a-hunting." "Alas!" she said, "I am the innocent cause of our sorrows," and told him of the exchange of the lamp. "Now I know," cried Aladdin, "that we have to thank the African magician for this! Where is the lamp?" "He carries it about with him," said the Princess. "I know, for he pulled it out of his breast to show me. He wishes me to break my faith with you and marry him, saying that you were beheaded by my father's command. He is forever speaking ill of you but I only reply by my tears. If I persist, I doubt not but he will use violence." Aladdin comforted her, and left her for a while. He changed clothes with the first person he met in the town, and having bought a certain powder, returned to the Princess, who let him in by a little side door. "Put on your most beautiful dress," he said to her, "and receive the magician with smiles, leading him to believe that you have forgotten me. Invite him to sup with you, and say you wish to taste the wine of his country. He will go for some and while he is gone I will tell you what to do." She listened carefully to Aladdin and when he left she arrayed herself gaily for the first time since she left China. She put on a girdle and head-dress of diamonds, and, seeing in a glass that she was more beautiful than ever, received the magician, saying, to his great amazement: "I have made up my mind that Aladdin is dead, and that all my tears will not bring him back to me, so I am resolved to mourn no more, and have therefore invited you to sup with me; but I am tired of the wines of China, and would fain taste those of Africa." The magician flew to his cellar, and the Princess put the powder Aladdin had given her in her cup. When he returned she asked him to drink her health in the wine of Africa, handing him her cup in exchange for his, as a sign she was reconciled to him. Before drinking the magician made her a speech in praise of her beauty, but the Princess cut him short, saying: "Let us drink first, and you shall say what you will afterward." She set her cup to her lips and kept it there, while the magician drained his to the dregs and fell back lifeless. The Princess then opened the door to Aladdin, and flung her arms round his neck; but Aladdin put her away, bidding her leave him, as he had more to do. He then went to the dead magician, took the lamp out of his vest, and bade the genie carry the palace and all in it back to China. This was done, and the Princess in her chamber only felt two little shocks, and little thought she was at home again.

The Sultan, who was sitting in his closet, mourning for his lost daughter, happened to look up, and rubbed his eyes, for there stood the palace as before! He hastened thither, and Aladdin received him in the hall of the four-and-twenty windows, with the Princess at his side. Aladdin told him what had happened, and showed him the dead body of the magician, that he might believe. A ten days' feast was proclaimed, and it seemed as if Aladdin might now live the rest of his life in peace; but it was not to be.

The African magician had a younger brother, who was, if possible, more wicked and more cunning than himself. He traveled to China to avenge his brother's death, and went to visit a pious woman called

Fatima, thinking she might be of use to him. He entered her cell and clapped a dagger to her breast, telling her to rise and do his bidding on pain of death. He changed clothes with her, colored his face like hers, put on her veil, and murdered her, that she might tell no tales. Then he went toward the palace of Aladdin, and all the people, thinking he was the holy woman, gathered round him, kissing his hands and begging his blessing. When he got to the palace there was such a noise going on round him that the Princess bade her slave look out of the window and ask what was the matter. The slave said it was the holy woman, curing people by her touch of their ailments, whereupon the Princess, who had long desired to see Fatima, sent for her. On coming to the Princess the magician offered up a prayer for her health and prosperity. When he had done the Princess made him sit by her, and begged him to stay with her always. The false Fatima, who wished for nothing better, consented, but kept his veil down for fear of discovery. The Princess showed him the hall, and asked him what he thought of it. "It is truly beautiful," said the false Fatima. "In my mind it wants but one thing." "And what is that?" said the Princess. "If only a roc's egg," replied he, "were hung up from the middle of this dome, it would be the wonder of the world."

After this the Princess could think of nothing but the roc's egg, and when Aladdin returned from hunting he found her in a very ill humor. He begged to know what was amiss, and she told him that all her pleasure in the hall was spoiled for the want of a roc's egg hanging from the dome. "If that is all," replied Aladdin, "you shall soon be happy." He left her and rubbed the lamp, and when the genie appeared commanded him to bring a roc's egg. The genie gave such a loud and terrible shriek that the hall shook. "Wretch!" he cried, "is it not enough that I have done everything for you, but you must command me to bring my master and hang him up in the midst of this dome? You and your wife and your palace deserve to be burnt to ashes, but that this request does not come from you, but from the brother of the African magician, whom you destroyed. He is now in your palace disguised as the holy woman—whom he murdered. He it was who put that wish into your wife's head. Take care of yourself, for he means to kill you." So saying, the genie disappeared.

Aladdin went back to the Princess, saying his head ached, and requesting that the holy Fatima should be fetched to lay her hands on it. But when the magician came near, Aladdin, seizing his dagger, pierced him to the heart. "What have you done?" cried the Princess. "You have killed the holy woman!" "Not so," replied Aladdin, "but a wicked magician," and told her of how she had been deceived.

After this Aladdin and his wife lived in peace. He succeeded the Sultan when he died, and reigned for many years, leaving behind him a long line of kings.

HOW TO MAKE SLIME

Be careful what surfaces the slime is placed on if you decide to make colored slime—food coloring could stain fabrics or furniture! Remember to wash your hands after playing.

WHAT YOU'LL NEED:

½ cup warm water

½ cup clear or white Elmer's Glue-All (about one 4-ounce bottle)

2 teaspoons Borax (laundry booster)

1 cup warm water

Food coloring (optional)

1. Mix the ½ cup of warm water and glue in one bowl (if you'd like a colored slime, add food coloring to the mixture at this point).
2. In another bowl, mix Borax together with one cup of warm water.
3. Pour the glue mixture into the Borax mixture and use your hands to combine the two. Now you're ready to play! You can store your slime in a sealed plastic sandwich bag to keep it from drying out.

Frère Jacques

Frère Jacques,
Frère Jacques,
Dormez-vous?
Dormez-vous?
Sonnez les matines,
Sonnez les matines.
Ding Ding Dong,
Ding Ding Dong.

Baa, Baa, Black Sheep

Baa, baa, black sheep,
Have you any wool?
Yes, sir, yes, sir,
Three bags full:
One for my master,
One for my dame,
And one for the little boy
Who lives in the lane.

JUST FOR LAUGHS

Trent: That sure is cool exercise equipment.

Matt: Thanks, I got it at the gym.

Trent: Did they have a sale?

Matt: No, they had a sign that said Free Weights.

Can an elephant jump higher than a house?

Of course. Houses can't jump at all.

Why did the cheerleading squad move into the haunted house?

Because it's got spirit!

Mona: What's worse than a giraffe with a sore throat?

Sam: A centipede with athlete's foot.

Mona: What kind of pet can help you write letters?

Sam: The alpha-pet.

"I can't remember what groceries I need," said Tom listlessly.

Didja hear about the police officer who arrested the young cat?

He saw the kitty litter.

Luna: How many seconds are in a year?

Larry: Twelve.

Luna: Only twelve! Are you sure?

Larry: Yeah, the second of January, the second of February . . .

Teacher: Tell me how you'd use the word "rhythm" in a sentence.

Alex: My older brother is going to the movies, and I want to go rhythm.

"Sir, do you believe in UFOs?"

"No comet."

Did you hear about the mad scientist who trained the Olympic diver?

He sent him off the deep end.

What do you call a tired tent?
A sleepy teepee.

Why is a baseball stadium such a cool place to be?
It's full of fans!

"I don't have a penny to my name."
"Are you gonna get a job?"
"No, I'm gonna change my name."

Doctor: Have your eyes ever been checked?
Kyle: No, they've always been blue.

Circus Clown: How do you like your new job?
Trapeze Artist: I'm finally getting the hang of things.

What happened to the origami store that used to be on the corner?
It folded.

Ben: Why are you jumping up and down?
Karl: I just took some medicine, and the bottle said to shake well.

Father: Go right up to your
  room and straighten it.
Jimmy: Is it crooked?

Why do they call her
  Strawberry?
She's good in a jam.

CLASSIC CARD GAME: SLAPJACK

*Slap the jack, and don't make the mistake of slapping another card!
If you're the first to slap a jack, you win all of the cards on the table.
The more cards you collect, the closer you are to winning the game.*

This game requires two to six players, and you'll
use a standard pack of fifty-two cards.

OBJECTIVE:

to collect the entire deck of cards, while develop-
ing awareness and fast response skills.

1. A random dealer is selected, and he deals out the entire deck evenly to
   all players, face down. You each make a neat stack with your cards and
   place the pile directly in front of you.
2. The game begins with each of you simultaneously turning over a card
   from your deck. If a jack is played, the first player to slap the card wins
   and collects all cards on the table. The player then places those cards
   at the bottom of her stack. You all continue to turn over the cards simultaneously until another jack is played.
3. If you run out of cards you can stay in the game by watching the others
   discard and being first to slap the jack. If you slap a card that is not a
   jack, you must give a card to each of the other players.
4. The game ends when one player has all of the cards.

HOW TO MAKE A PAPER AIRPLANE

Prepare for takeoff as you and your child investigate the art of making paper airplanes. Try this basic design and get ready to defy gravity!

WHAT YOU'LL NEED:

One 8½" × 11" sheet of paper (Almost any weight of paper will work, from computer paper to construction paper.)

A flat work surface and your hands!

1. Fold the paper exactly in half the long way, and re-open it, creating two halves. The center line crease will be your guideline.
2. Position your unfolded paper flat in front of you so that the crease runs vertically. Take the top end of the paper and fold each of the two corners in towards the center so that the inside edges line up with the center line crease.
3. Fold the paper down on each side again so that the inside edges line up with the center crease.
4. Turn the paper airplane over and fold it in half again along the center line. You will now be looking at your plane from the side.
5. To make the wings, fold the upper edges down from the top of the plane, lining up the top fold with the center line (your original center fold is now the bottom of the plane). Turn over the plane and repeat on the other side to make the second wing.
6. You can also experiment with adding different folds in the wings of your plane or with the angles you throw your airplane! Get ready to fly!

I've Been Working on the Railroad

I've been working on the railroad
All the livelong day
I've been working on the railroad
Just to pass the time away

Can't you hear the whistle blowing
Rise up so early in the morn
Can't you hear the captain shouting
Dinah, blow your horn

Dinah, won't you blow
Dinah, won't you blow
Dinah, won't you blow your horn
Dinah, won't you blow
Dinah, won't you blow
Dinah, won't you blow your horn

Someone's in the kitchen with Dinah
Someone's in the kitchen I know
Someone's in the kitchen with Dinah
Strumming on the old banjo, and singing

Fee, fi, fiddly-i-o
Fee, fi, fiddly-i-o
Fee, fi, fiddly-i-o
Strumming on the old banjo

Blue Beard

BY CHARLES PERRAULT

THERE WAS A MAN who had fine houses, both in town and country, a deal of silver and gold plate, embroidered furniture, and coaches gilded all over with gold. But this man had the misfortune to have a blue beard, which made him so frightfully ugly, that all the women and girls ran away from him.

One of his neighbors, a lady of quality, had two daughters who were perfect beauties. He desired of her one of them in marriage, leaving to her the choice which of the two she would bestow upon him. They would neither of them have him, and each made the other welcome of him, being not able to bear the thought of marrying a man who had a blue beard. And what besides gave them disgust and aversion, was his having already been married to several wives, and nobody ever knew what became of them.

Blue Beard, to engage their affection, took them, with the lady their mother, and three or four ladies of their acquaintance, with other young people of the neighborhood, to one of his country seats, where they stayed a whole week. There was nothing then to be seen but parties of pleasure, hunting, fishing, dancing, mirth, and feasting. Nobody went to bed, but all passed the night in playing tricks upon each other. In short, every thing succeeded so well, that the youngest daughter began to think the master of the house not to have a beard so very blue, and that he was a mighty civil gentleman. As soon as they returned home, the marriage was concluded.

About a month afterwards Blue Beard told his wife that he was obliged to take a country journey for six weeks at least, about affairs of very great consequence, desiring her to divert herself in his absence, to send for her friends and acquaintances, to carry them into the country, if she pleased, and to make good cheer wherever she was.

"Here," said he, "are the keys of the two great wardrobes, wherein I have my best furniture; these are of my silver and gold plate, which is not every day in use; these open my strong boxes, which hold my money, both gold and silver; these my caskets of jewels; and this is the master-key to all my apartments. But for this little one here, it is the key of the closet at the end of the great gallery on the ground floor. Open them all; go into all and every one of them; except that little closet which I forbid you, and forbid it in such a manner that, if you happen to open it, there will be no bounds to my just anger and resentment."

She promised to observe, very exactly, whatever he had ordered; when he, after having embraced her, got into his coach and proceeded on his journey.

Her neighbors and good friends did not stay to be sent for by the new-married lady, so great was their impatience to see all the rich furniture of her house, not daring to come while her husband was there, because of his blue beard which frightened them. They ran through all the rooms, closets, and wardrobes, which were all so rich and fine, that they seemed to surpass one another.

After that, they went up into the two great rooms, where were the best and richest furniture; they could not sufficiently admire the number and beauty of the tapestry, beds, couches, cabinets, stands, tables, and looking-glasses in which you might see yourself from head to foot; some of them were framed with glass, others with silver, plain and gilded, the finest and most magnificent which were ever seen. They ceased not to extol and envy the happiness of their friend, who in the mean time no way diverted herself in looking upon all these rich things, because of the impatience she had to go and open the closet of the ground floor. She was so much pressed by her curiosity, that, without considering that it was very uncivil to leave her company, she went down a little back staircase, and with such excessive haste, that she had twice or thrice like to have broken her neck.

Being come to the closet door, she made a stop for some time, thinking upon her husband's orders, and considering what unhappiness might attend her if she was disobedient; but the temptation was so strong she could not overcome it. She took then the little key, and opened it trembling; but could not at first see any thing plainly, because the windows were shut. After some moments she began to perceive that the floor was all covered over with clotted blood, in which were reflected the bodies of several dead women ranged against the walls: these were all the wives whom Blue Beard had married and murdered one after another. She was like to have died for fear, and the key, which she pulled out of the lock, fell out of her hand.

After having somewhat recovered her senses, she took up the key, locked the door, and went up stairs into her chamber to recover herself; but she could not, so much was she frightened. Having observed that the key of the closet was stained with blood, she tried two or three times to wipe it off, but the blood would not come off; in vain did she wash it, and even rub it with soap and sand, the blood still remained, for the key was magical, and she could never make it quite clean; when the blood was gone off from one side, it came again on the other.

Blue Beard returned from his journey the same evening, and said, he had received letters upon the road, informing him that the affair he went about was ended to his advantage. His wife did all she could to convince him she was extremely glad of his speedy return. Next morning he asked her for the keys, which she gave him, but with such a trembling hand, that he easily guessed what had happened.

"What," said he, "is not the key of my closet among the rest?"

"I must certainly," answered she, "have left it above upon the table."

"Fail not," said Blue Beard, "to bring it me presently."

After putting him off several times, she was forced to bring him the key. Blue Beard, having very attentively considered it, said to his wife:

"How comes this blood upon the key?"

"I do not know," cried the poor woman, paler than death.

"You do not know," replied Blue Beard; "I very well know, you were resolved to go into the closet, were you not? Mighty well, Madam; you shall go in, and take your place among the ladies you saw there."

Upon this she threw herself at her husband's feet, and begged his pardon with all the signs of a true repentance for her disobedience. She would have melted a rock, so beautiful and sorrowful was she; but Blue Beard had a heart harder than any rock.

"You must die, Madam," said he, "and that presently."

"Since I must die," answered she, looking upon him with her eyes all bathed in tears, "give me some little time to say my prayers."

"I give you," replied Blue Beard, "half a quarter of an hour, but not one moment more."

When she was alone, she called out to her sister, and said to her:

"Sister Anne" (for that was her name), "go up I beg you, upon the top of the tower, and look if my brothers are not coming; they promised me that they would come today, and if you see them, give them a sign to make haste."

Her sister Anne went up upon the top of the tower, and the poor afflicted wife cried out from time to time, "Anne, sister Anne, do you see any one coming?"

And sister Anne said:

"I see nothing but the sun, which makes a dust, and the grass growing green."

In the mean while Blue Beard, holding a great scimitar in his hand, cried out as loud as he could bawl to his wife:

"Come down instantly, or I shall come up to you."

"One moment longer, if you please," said his wife, and then she cried out very softly:

"Anne, sister Anne, dost thou see anybody coming?"

And sister Anne answered:

"I see nothing but the sun, which makes a dust, and the grass growing green."

"Come down quickly," cried Blue Beard, "or I will come up to you."

"I am coming," answered his wife; and then she cried:

"Anne, sister Anne, dost thou see anyone coming?"

"I see," replied sister Anne, "a great dust that comes this way."

"Are they my brothers?"

"Alas! no, my dear sister, I see a flock of sheep."

"Will you not come down?" cried Blue Beard.

"One moment longer," said his wife, and then she cried out:

"Anne, sister Anne, dost thou see nobody coming?"

"I see," said she, "two horsemen coming, but they are yet a great way off."

"God be praised," she cried presently, "they are my brothers; I am beckoning to them, as well as I can, for them to make haste."

Then Blue Beard bawled out so loud, that he made the whole house tremble. The distressed wife came down, and threw herself at his feet, all in tears, with her hair about her shoulders.

"Nought will avail," said Blue Beard, "you must die"; then, taking hold of her hair with one hand, and lifting up his scimitar with the other, he was going to take off her head.

The poor lady turning about to him, and looking at him with dying eyes, desired him to afford her one little moment to recollect herself.

"No, no," said he, "recommend thyself to God," and was just ready to strike.

At this very instant there was such a loud knocking at the gate, that Blue Beard made a sudden stop. The gate was opened, and presently entered two horsemen, who drawing their swords, ran directly to Blue Beard. He knew them to be his wife's brothers, one a dragoon, the other a musketeer; so that he ran away immediately to save himself; but the two brothers pursued so close, that they overtook him before he could get to the steps of the porch, when they ran their swords through his body and left him dead. The poor wife was almost as dead as her husband, and had not strength enough to rise and welcome her brothers.

Blue Beard had no heirs, and so his wife became mistress of all his estate. She made use of one part of it to marry her sister Anne to a young gentleman who had loved her a long while; another part to buy captains' commissions for her brothers; and the rest to marry herself to a very worthy gentleman, who made her forget the ill time she had passed with Blue Beard.

Where Go the Boats?

BY ROBERT LOUIS STEVENSON

Dark brown is the river,
Golden is the sand.
It flows along for ever,
With trees on either hand.

Green leaves a-floating,
Castles of the foam,
Boats of mine a-boating—
Where will all come home?

On goes the river
And out past the mill,
Away down the valley,
Away down the hill.

Away down the river,
A hundred miles or more,
Other little children
Shall bring my boats ashore.

Rumpelstiltskin

BY THE GRIMM BROTHERS

B y the side of a wood, in a country a long way off, ran a fine stream of water; and upon the stream there stood a mill. The miller's house was close by, and the miller, you must know, had a very beautiful daughter. She was, moreover, very shrewd and clever; and the miller was so proud of her, that he one day told the king of the land, who used to come and hunt in the wood, that his daughter could spin gold out of straw. Now this king was very fond of money; and when he heard the miller's boast his greediness was raised, and he sent for the girl to be brought before him. Then he led her to a chamber in his palace where there was a great heap of straw, and gave her a spinning-wheel, and said, "All this must be spun into gold before morning, as you love your life." It was in vain that the poor maiden said that it was only a silly boast of her father, for that she could do no such thing as spin straw into gold: the chamber door was locked, and she was left alone.

She sat down in one corner of the room, and began to bewail her hard fate; when on a sudden the door opened, and a droll-looking little man hobbled in, and said, "Good morrow to you, my good lass; what are you weeping for?" "Alas!" said she, "I must spin this straw into gold, and I know not how." "What will you give me," said the hobgoblin, "to do it for you?" "My necklace," replied the maiden. He took her at her word, and sat himself down to the wheel, and whistled and sang:

"Round about, round about,

Lo and behold!

Reel away, reel away,

Straw into gold!"

And round about the wheel went merrily; the work was quickly done, and the straw was all spun into gold.

When the king came and saw this, he was greatly astonished and pleased; but his heart grew still more greedy of gain, and he shut up the poor miller's daughter again with a fresh task. Then she knew not what to do, and sat down once more to weep; but the dwarf soon opened the door, and said, "What will you give me to do your task?" "The ring on my finger," said she. So her little friend took the ring, and began to work at the wheel again, and whistled and sang:

"Round about, round about,

Lo and behold!

Reel away, reel away,

Straw into gold!"

Till, long before morning, all was done again.

The king was greatly delighted to see all this glittering treasure; but still he had not enough: so he took the miller's daughter to a yet larger heap, and said, "All this must be spun tonight; and if it is, you shall be my queen." As soon as she was alone that dwarf came in, and said, "What will you give me to spin gold for you this third time?" "I have nothing left," said she. "Then say you will give me," said the little man, "the first little child that you may have when you are queen." "That may never be," thought the miller's daughter: and as she knew no other way to get her task done, she said she would do what he asked. Round went the wheel again to the old song, and the manikin once more spun the heap into gold. The king came in the morning, and, finding all he wanted, was forced to keep his word; so he married the miller's daughter, and she really became queen.

At the birth of her first little child she was very glad, and forgot the dwarf, and what she had said. But one day he came into her room, where she was sitting playing with her baby, and put her in mind of it. Then she grieved sorely at her misfortune, and said she would give him all the wealth of the kingdom if he would let her off, but in vain; till at last her tears softened him, and he said, "I will give you three days' grace, and if during that time you tell me my name, you shall keep your child."

Now the queen lay awake all night, thinking of all the odd names that she had ever heard; and she sent messengers all over the land to find out new ones. The next day the little man came, and she began with Timothy, Ichabod, Benjamin, Jeremiah, and all the names she could remember; but to all and each of them he said, "Madam, that is not my name."

The second day she began with all the comical names she could hear of, Bandy-Legs, Hunchback, Crook-Shanks, and so on; but the little gentleman still said to every one of them, "Madam, that is not my name."

The third day one of the messengers came back, and said, "I have traveled two days without hearing of any other names; but yesterday, as I was climbing a high hill, among the trees of the forest where the fox and the hare bid each other good night, I saw a little hut; and before the hut burnt a fire; and round about the fire a funny little dwarf was dancing upon one leg, and singing:

'Merrily the feast I'll make.
Today I'll brew, tomorrow bake;
Merrily I'll dance and sing,
For next day will a stranger bring.
Little does my lady dream
Rumpelstiltskin is my name!'"

When the queen heard this she jumped for joy, and as soon as her little friend came she sat down upon her throne, and called all her court round to enjoy the fun; and the nurse stood by her side with the baby in her arms, as if it was quite ready to be given up. Then the little man began to chuckle at the thought of having the poor child, to take home with him to his hut in the woods; and he cried out, "Now, lady, what is my name?" "Is it John?" asked she. "No, madam!" "Is it Tom?" "No, madam!" "Is it Jemmy?" "It is not." "Can your name be *Rumpel-stiltskin*?" said the lady slyly. "Some witch told you that!—some witch told you that!" cried the little man, and dashed his right foot in a rage so deep into the floor, that he was forced to lay hold of it with both hands to pull it out.

Then he made the best of his way off, while the nurse laughed and the baby crowed; and all the court jeered at him for having had so much trouble for nothing, and said, "We wish you a very good morning, and a merry feast, Mr. Rumpelstiltskin!"

To an Insect

BY OLIVER WENDELL HOLMES

I love to hear thine earnest voice,
    Wherever thou art hid,
Thou testy little dogmatist,
    Thou pretty Katydid!
Thou mindest me of gentlefolks, —
    Old gentlefolks are they, —
Thou say'st an undisputed thing
    In such a solemn way.

Thou art a female, Katydid!
    I know it by the trill
That quivers through thy piercing notes,
    So petulant and shrill,
I think there is a knot of you
    Beneath the hollow tree, —
A knot of spinster Katydids, —
    Do Katydids drink tea?

Oh, tell me where did Katy live,
    And what did Katy do?
And was she very fair and young,
    And yet so wicked, too?
Did Katy love a naughty man,
    Or kiss more cheeks than one?
I warrant Katy did no more
    Than many a Kate has done.

Dear me! I'll tell you all about
My fuss with little Jane,
And Ann, with whom I used to walk
So often down the lane,
And all that tore their locks of black,
Or wet their eyes of blue, —
Pray tell me, sweetest Katydid,
What did poor Katy do?

Ah no! the living oak shall crash,
That stood for ages still,
The rock shall rend its mossy base
And thunder down the hill,
Before the little Katydid
Shall add one word, to tell
The mystic story of the maid
Whose name she knows so well.

Peace to the ever murmuring race!
And when the latest one
Shall fold in death her feeble wings
Beneath the autumn sun,
Then shall she raise her fainting voice,
And lift her drooping lid,
And then the child of future years
Shall hear what Katy did.

The Elves and the Shoemaker

BY THE GRIMM BROTHERS

There was once a shoemaker, who worked very hard and was very honest: but still he could not earn enough to live upon; and at last all he had in the world was gone, save just leather enough to make one pair of shoes.

Then he cut his leather out, all ready to make up the next day, meaning to rise early in the morning to his work. His conscience was clear and his heart light amidst all his troubles; so he went peaceably to bed, left all his cares to Heaven, and soon fell asleep. In the morning after he had said his prayers, he sat himself down to his work; when, to his great wonder, there stood the shoes all ready made, upon the table. The good man knew not what to say or think at such an odd thing happening. He looked at the workmanship; there was not one false stitch in the whole job; all was so neat and true, that it was quite a masterpiece.

The same day a customer came in, and the shoes suited him so well that he willingly paid a price higher than usual for them; and the poor shoemaker, with the money, bought leather enough to make two pairs more. In the evening he cut out the work, and went to bed early, that he might get up and begin betimes next day; but he was saved all the trouble, for when he got up in the morning the work was done ready to his hand. Soon in came buyers, who paid him handsomely for his goods, so that he bought leather enough for four pair more. He cut out the work again overnight and found it done in the morning, as before;

and so it went on for some time: what was got ready in the evening was always done by daybreak, and the good man soon became thriving and well off again.

One evening, about Christmas-time, as he and his wife were sitting over the fire chatting together, he said to her, "I should like to sit up and watch tonight, that we may see who it is that comes and does my work for me." The wife liked the thought; so they left a light burning, and hid themselves in a corner of the room, behind a curtain that was hung up there, and watched what would happen.

As soon as it was midnight, there came in two little naked dwarfs; and they sat themselves upon the shoemaker's bench, took up all the work that was cut out, and began to ply with their little fingers, stitching and rapping and tapping away at such a rate, that the shoemaker was all wonder, and could not take his eyes off them. And on they went, till the job was quite done, and the shoes stood ready for use upon the table. This was long before daybreak; and then they bustled away as quick as lightning.

The next day the wife said to the shoemaker, "These little wights have made us rich, and we ought to be thankful to them, and do them a good turn if we can. I am quite sorry to see them run about as they do; and indeed it is not very decent, for they have nothing upon their backs to keep off the cold. I'll tell you what, I will make each of them a shirt, and a coat and waistcoat, and a pair of pantaloons into the bargain; and do you make each of them a little pair of shoes."

The thought pleased the good cobbler very much; and one evening, when all the things were ready, they laid them on the table, instead of the work that they used to cut out, and then went and hid themselves, to watch what the little elves would do.

About midnight in they came, dancing and skipping, hopped round the room, and then went to sit down to their work as usual; but when they saw the clothes lying for them, they laughed and chuckled, and seemed mightily delighted.

Then they dressed themselves in the twinkling of an eye, and danced and capered and sprang about, as merry as could be; till at last they danced out at the door, and away over the green.

The good couple saw them no more; but everything went well with them from that time forward, as long as they lived.

JUST FOR LAUGHS

Knock knock.
Who's there?
Iguanodon.
Iguanodon who?
Iguanodon town to see the
   dinosaur exhibit.

"A train smashed into my
   bicycle, and I didn't even
   get hurt."
"Why not?"
"My brother Dave was rid-
   ing it."

A college star fullback played
   with his team for 12 years!
He could run and tackle—he
   just couldn't pass.

A rookie cop got bawled out
   by his sergeant after working his first stakeout.
"How could you let that crook
   escape?" yelled the sergeant. "I told you to keep
   an eye on all the exits."
"I did, Sarge. He must
   have gone out one of the
   entrances."

A flea and a fly in a flue
Were imprisoned so what
  could they do?
Said the fly, "Let us flee,"
Said the flea, "Let us fly,"
So they flew through a flaw
  in the flue.

Why do they call him
  Needles?
He's so sharp.

Why do they call him Buck?
He's got a *lot* of cents.

Megan: I think my mom must
  be the strongest person in
  the world.
Troy: Why do you say that?
Megan: Because every day
  she picks up my entire
  room using only her bare
  hands.

The animal doctor is always busy as a bee! Take a gander at a few of his patients:
The leopard is seeing spots,
The kangaroo is feeling jumpy,
The goldfish is flushed,
The chameleon is looking green,
The woodpecker caught a bug,
The baby duckling has been getting a little down lately,
And the bullfrog is afraid he's going to croak!

Jimmy: We got a brand new roof and it didn't cost us a cent!
Megan: Why not?
Jimmy: The carpenters told us it was on the house.

What weighs 2,000 pounds, has big ears, tusks, and two trunks?
An elephant going on vacation.

"George Washington's parents were really thoughtful."
"What makes you say that?"
"They made sure their kid was born on a holiday."

A father saw his son out in the backyard cleaning their homemade swing, a rubber tire hanging by a rope from a tree branch. The son was hosing it down, wiping it off, dusting out the inside. The puzzled father went outside and said, "Son, I thought you were playing on the golf course with your friends this afternoon." "I was," replied the boy. "But the golf instructor said I needed to improve my swing."

Why does your dog go round and round before he lies down?
He's a self-winding watchdog.

Sam: I haven't seen your pet chicken lately.
Mona: Well, this week she's been laying low.

The Land of Counterpane

BY ROBERT LOUIS STEVENSON

When I was sick and lay a-bed,
I had two pillows at my head,
And all my toys beside me lay,
To keep me happy all the day.

And sometimes for an hour or so
I watched my leaden soldiers go,
With different uniforms and drills,
Among the bedclothes, through the hills;

And sometimes sent my ships in fleets
All up and down among the sheets;
Or brought my trees and houses out,
And planted cities all about.

I was the giant great and still
That sits upon the pillow-hill,
And sees before him, dale and plain,
The pleasant land of counterpane.

The Leaping Match

BY HANS CHRISTIAN ANDERSEN

The Flea, the Grasshopper, and the Frog once wanted to see which of them could jump the highest. They made a festival, and invited the whole world and every one else besides who liked to come and see the grand sight. Three famous jumpers they were, as all should say, when they met together in the room.

"I will give my daughter to him who shall jump highest," said the King; "it would be too bad for you to have the jumping, and for us to offer no prize."

The Flea was the first to come forward. He had most exquisite manners, and bowed to the company on every side; for he was of noble blood, and, besides, was accustomed to the society of man, and that, of course, had been an advantage to him.

Next came the Grasshopper. He was not quite so elegantly formed as the Flea, but he knew perfectly well how to conduct himself, and he wore the green uniform which belonged to him by right of birth. He said, moreover, that he came of a very ancient Egyptian family, and that in the house where he then lived he was much thought of.

The fact was that he had been just brought out of the fields and put in a card-house three stories high, and built on purpose for him, with the colored sides inwards, and doors and windows cut out of the Queen of Hearts. "And I sing so well," said he, "that sixteen parlor-bred crickets, who have chirped from infancy and yet got no one to build them card-houses to live in, have fretted themselves thinner even than before, from sheer vexation on hearing me."

It was thus that the Flea and the Grasshopper made the most of themselves, each thinking himself quite an equal match for the princess.

The Leapfrog said not a word; but people said that perhaps he thought the more; and the housedog who snuffed at him with his nose allowed that he was of good family. The old councilor, who had had three orders given him in vain for keeping quiet, asserted that the Leapfrog was a prophet, for that one could see on his back whether the coming winter was to be severe or mild, which is more than one can see on the back of the man who writes the almanac.

"I say nothing for the present," exclaimed the King; "yet I have my own opinion, for I observe everything."

And now the match began. The Flea jumped so high that no one could see what had become of him; and so they insisted that he had not jumped at all—which was disgraceful after all the fuss he had made.

The Grasshopper jumped only half as high; but he leaped into the King's face, who was disgusted by his rudeness.

The Leapfrog stood for a long time, as if lost in thought; people began to think he would not jump at all.

"I'm afraid he is ill!" said the dog and he went to snuff at him again; when lo! he suddenly made a sideways jump into the lap of the princess, who sat close by on a little golden stool.

"There is nothing higher than my daughter," said the King; "therefore to bound into her lap is the highest jump that can be made. Only one of good understanding would ever have thought of that. Thus the Frog has shown that he has sense. He has brains in his head, that he has."

And so he won the princess.

"I jumped the highest, for all that," said the Flea; "but it's all the same to me. The princess may have the stiff-legged, slimy creature, if she likes. In this world merit seldom meets its reward. Dullness and heaviness win the day. I am too light and airy for a stupid world."

And so the Flea went into foreign service.

The Grasshopper sat without on a green bank and reflected on the world and its ways; and he too said, "Yes, dullness and heaviness win the day; a fine exterior is what people care for nowadays." And then he began to sing in his own peculiar way—and it is from his song that we have taken this little piece of history, which may very possibly be all untrue, although it does stand printed here in black and white.

HOW TO SAY "I LOVE YOU" IN DIFFERENT LANGUAGES

You probably say "I love you" countless times a day. Why not mix it up once in awhile with a foreign language version?

- Afrikaans: Ek het jou lief
- Albanian: Te dua
- Armenian: Yes kez si'rumem
- Cantonese: Ngo oi ney
- Creole: Mi aime jou
- Danish: Jeg elsker dig
- Dutch: Ik hou van jou
- English: I love you
- Filipino: Iniibig kita
- Finnish: Mina rakastan sinua
- French: Je t'aime
- German: Ich liebe dich
- Greek: S'agapo
- Hawaiian: Aloha wau `iâ `oe
- Hungarian: Szeretlek te'ged
- Icelandic: Eg elska thig
- Indonesian: Saya cinta padamu
- Irish/Gaelic: Taim i' ngra leat
- Italian: Ti amo
- Japanese: Kimi o ai shiteru
- Korean: Dangsinul saranghee yo
- Malaysian: Saya cinta mu
- Mandarin: Wo ay ni
- Norwegian: Jeg elsker deg
- Polish: Kocham cie
- Portuguese (Brazilian): Eu te amo
- Romanian: Te iubesc
- Russian: Ya lyublyu tyebya
- Spanish: Te amo
- Swahili: Nakupenda
- Swedish: Jag älskar dig
- Ukrainian: Ya tebe kokhaju
- Vietnamese: Toi yeu em

JUST FOR LAUGHS

Didja hear about the taxicab driver who lost his job?
He was driving away all his customers.

Didja hear about the pet-shop owner who couldn't sell his porcupine?
He was stuck with it.

Larry: How many feet are in a yard?
Luna: That depends on how many people are standing in it.

The bottle of perfume that Willie sent
Was highly displeasing to Millicent.
Her thanks were so cold
That they quarreled, I'm told,
'Bout that silly scent Willie sent Millicent.

First Fisher: Is this a good lake for fish?
Second Fisher: It must be. I can't get any of them to come out.

Luna: My candy bar is missing.
Larry: That's too bad, because it tasted delicious.

Did you hear about the lobster that bought a new car? It was a crustacean wagon.

"My aunt always nagged my uncle to buy her a Jaguar."
"Did he ever get one?"
"Yeah, then it ate her up!"

Luna: Do you know how long the world's longest nose was?
Larry: Eleven inches.
Luna: That's not very long.
Larry: If it was any longer it would be a foot.

Astronaut: What are you digging in your pockets for?
Astronaut: You said we'd be landing this thing at a meteor, and most parking meteors only take quarters.

Did you hear about the poor little baby who stayed with the mad scientist? It went ga-ga.

Knock knock.
Who's there?
Champ.
Champ who?
Champoo the dog, he's got fleas!

"Young man, there were two cookies in the jar last night, and this morning there is only one. How do you explain that?"
"It was so dark, I guessed I missed it."

Larry: Why don't we fall off the earth and go shooting through space?
Perry: The law of gravity.

Larry: Then what did we do before that law was passed?

At a fancy hotel, a man walks in and asks the desk clerk, "Do you take children?"
"No sir," replied the clerk. "Only credit cards."

Knock knock.
Who's there?
Boo.
Boo who?
Why are you crying?

At the airport, Mother turned to Father and said, "I sure wish we had brought the television with us."

"Why is that?" asked Father.

"Because I left the plane tickets on it."

What do you get if you cross a hill with an electric stove?

A mountain range.

Mother: What's your little brother yelling about?

Sandy: I don't know. I let him lick the beater after I made peanut butter fudge. Maybe I should have turned it off first.

"Having children is like living in a frat house— nobody sleeps, everything's broken, and there's a lot of throwing up."

—RAY ROMANO

SAY BEDTIME PRAYERS

There's nothing sweeter than watching your children say a bedtime prayer.

Grace

BY E. RUTTER LEATHAM

Thank you for the world so sweet,
Thank you for the food we eat.
Thank you for the birds that sing,
Thank you, God, for everything.

A Child's Evening Hymn

I hear no voice, I feel no touch,
I see no glory bright;
But yet I know that God is near,
In darkness as in light.
God watches ever by my side,
And hears my whispered prayer:
A God of love for a little child
Both night and day does care.

Now I Lay Me Down

Now I lay me down to sleep,
I pray the Lord my soul to keep,
Lord, be with me through the night
And keep me 'til the morning light.

Angel Blessing at Bedtime

Angels bless and angels keep
Angels guard me while I sleep
Bless my heart and bless my home
Bless my spirit as I roam
Guide and guard me through the night
And wake me with the morning's light.
Amen.

Printed in the United States
By Bookmasters